'BEEF'

JOHN TORODE

'BEEF'

and other bovine matters

photographs by Jason Lowe

The Taunton Press

'INTRODUCTION'

When I opened Smiths of Smithfield, in London in 2000, I was already well into my love affair with all things beef, but eight years on the relationship is now well and truly cemented. It is the one subject I can discuss till the cows come home (ho ho), but it is also an area that many people feel very confused about—both in what to buy, and then how to get the best out of the meat they have bought. After many years of thinking about it and discussing it, here it is: the cookbook I felt compelled to write. It's aimed at everyone—home cooks as well as chefs.

BEEF has been written because I believe that good food should be accessible to all people. That is the simple reason. I hope it will give you the confidence not just to cook beef but also to buy beef and recognize what is good and, more importantly, what ain't.

When given the chance to write this book, I really wanted to pour out all I know and love about beef. I have tried to be as helpful as possible without being a food bore or getting too technical; I don't want the book to be scary, so I have given just as much advice as is practical. At the least, you will find a huge range of recipes, cooking tips, and advice on how to buy good beef, and that is the best start.

The bottom line is good food, food that people want to eat. Some recipes are 15-minute wonders and some will be more involved—it would not be a good book if they were not!

Most, though, are mine, learned from simple home cooking, because right or wrong I feel restaurant recipes belong in a restaurant. Restaurant chefs cook differently; their kitchens are run differently; their recipes are practiced and concise, and leave little room for messing around. I am not precious—if you want to add something or take something away, go for it. Change the recipes, have fun, and if anything works better than my recipe, send me a note. I shall burn it! (Just joking—I would appreciate it. We all need to learn new tricks.)

Food, cooking, kitchens, friends, dinner tables—they are good things, but good things are not always constant. Good food moves and changes, depending on your mood, your friends—even the weather can affect it. If we are honest, we all have our "best" recipes. Whether it is a great salad, a chargrilled burger, or a beautiful pastry dish like Beef Wellington, the recipe has generally taken a lot of practice to reach what we feel is perfection. What I'm saying is: If a recipe in this book doesn't turn out so well for you one day, don't dismiss it. Give it another try.

Finally, a few general points on the recipes. Assume eggs are large and pepper is black and freshly milled unless the recipe says otherwise; measure cups and spoons level unless it says "heaped." The cow symbols 🐄 under each recipe title indicate how many people the dish will serve. An outlined symbol indicates a half portion.

'SOME BASICS'

Beef is for eating and comes from beef cattle. Milk comes from dairy cows. Dairy cows are primarily those black and white ones that look like they are having fun, whereas beef cattle are most of the beautiful big butch ones that stand and stare at you.

THE BULL: the male. He is there to breed—that's his job. Older ones are not eaten, because they are as tough as old boots.

THE STEER: a castrated bull, used for beef production. He can't do much but eat and sleep, poor fellow.

THE HEIFER: a female. They give birth each year, but a heifer is primarily for beef production. She gets to play with the bull.

THE COW: a female used for dairy—that is, milking. They are usually Holsteins and have udders. The meat from them is not too good, hence the expression "old cow."

VEAL: the male calves from a dairy herd. As I have said above, dairy cattle don't grow into great beef, but if slaughtered young they do make great veal.

So much of what I have read about beef is aimed at the lucky few who can afford to spend lots of money at top butchers, farmers' markets, or online shopping. Good meat is not cheap, but it should not break the bank either. There are plenty of retailers who are more than willing to give you sound advice to add to mine about what meat you should buy for a particular dish. There are a few simple rules:

All meat is muscle; each muscle works at a different rate and holds a different weight.

The muscles that do all the work, such as lower leg (shank) and shoulder (chuck), need long, slow cooking to break down the tissue. These cuts should always be served well done.

The muscles that do less work, such as upper leg (round), will be more tender and can be broiled, grilled, and fried, but slowly, not quickly. When cooked that bit longer, to medium, they will be more tender.

The muscles that do no work, such as the short loin and rib, can be cooked quickly to be served rare, because they do not have the structure of a working muscle.

The very best beef, regardless of where on the beast it is from, should have fine rivers of fat running through the muscle so that, as it cooks, the fat melts and keeps the meat moist. The greater the marbling of fat, the higher the grade. Prime, the highest of the eight USDA grades (usually reserved for restaurants), goes to well-marbled meat from specially raised cattle. Most of the meat found in supermarkets is Choice, the second highest grade; this has minimal to moderate marbling.

A good beef animal will be 18 to 24 months old. It should have had a nice life, grazing calmly on grass, free of stress, until being grown to maturity ("finished") in feedlots. It should have a well-formed body but, unlike an athlete, would have had time to lay fat in the muscle. An animal that's been worked will be tough, regardless of how long you cook it.

The last part of its life is important too. A great animal will be ruined if its slaughter is stressful. A stressed kill pumps adrenalin into the blood, reducing the flesh to grainy, chewy, watery lumps of bitter meat.

Value

The value of each cut is determined by customer demand. In Asia, offal is extremely expensive because people prize it, whereas in the West tenderloin is highly prized. (In reality there are far better cuts than tenderloin; you just have to know how to cook them.) It is all about supply and demand—there are only two tenderloins of, say, 6 to 8 pounds each in a beast, so they are a rarity, whereas 90 pounds of chuck is not as scarce and so not as expensive.

Flavor

The most worked (and well-lived) muscles will deliver the best flavor, until you start to take aging into account. However, the rule of thumb is that the brisket, for example, will taste a lot richer than the rib or tenderloin.

Aging

This is the technique used to tenderize beef and develop the flavor. I only like beef that is dry-aged, because it is so tender with the most fantastic flavor. In dry-aging the meat remains attached to the bone and hangs, as a carcass or large cut, in a cooler for up to six weeks, during which time it loses moisture and the natural flavor is concentrated. For wet-aging (also called aging in the bag)—which is what is used for most beef—the cuts are packed inside vacuum-sealed plastic bags. They do age, and become more tender, but don't lose moisture as they do with dry-aging. So I don't think the flavor is anywhere near as good.

'BUYING BEEF'

I believe it is important to know where your beast comes from, what it has been fed, and how it has lived. So, in all the time I have been seriously buying beef, I have supported the Rare Breeds Survival Trust, a conservation charity devoted to Britain's native livestock breeds. It is a group of great farmers, breeders, and producers—I like the people I buy from.

Let's make no bones about it, this meat is expensive, but quality delivers yield. The meat from an animal that has reached its full lifecycle and is treated well, then hung and dry-aged will be worth every penny.

My advice is, if at all possible, try to find a skilled butcher you can get to know and trust. This really helps when buying any type of meat. As you build a relationship with your butcher, he will point you toward the best cuts and specials in any given season. If he dry-ages his beef, you'll be even more fortunate.

Having said that, I am also a realist. I know that most beef today is shipped as "boxed beef" (boxes of vacuum-packed, wet-aged cuts), which retailers keep refrigerated until the bag is opened and the beef is cut for sale, and that most people buy their beef from supermarkets. With this in mind, throughout the book I've given you lots of hints and tips. They are not there to scare you, but to inform and educate. This is a cookbook after all, not a lecture.

Organic beef is from cattle born and raised on a certified organic farm, where they are given 100 percent organic feed (whether grass or grain) and have unrestricted outdoor access. The cattle are not given antibiotics to control disease or hormones to promote growth.

So-called "natural" beef is not the same as organic, although the two terms are often used interchangeably. Although natural beef producers may choose not to use antibiotics routinely to prevent disease or steroids to promote growth, there is no USDA verification system for natural beef as there is for organic.

'THE BREEDS'

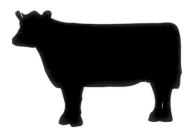

Aberdeen Angus

The true Aberdeen Angus has a smooth, solid black coat. The bull is huge and majestic, and has been the pride of Scotland, but unfortunately few pure breeds now exist. They are slow growers, and the promotion of Angus as great for eating has lead to commercial cross-breeding. It's a shame. The few times I have eaten true Angus it has been a good hunk of beef.

Belgian Blue

This is the body builder of beef cattle and also bred for milk production. It is a massive animal (thankfully with a quiet temperament) and has an all-white coat with a blue tinge and a stance like a bulldog.

Beefmaster

Now recognized as a true breed, the Beefmaster is a cross between the Hereford, the Shorthorn, and the Brahman. It is usually light to dark red and medium size compared to other cattle breeds, and has a gentle nature.

Brahman

These cattle have a very distinctive appearance, with a large hump above their shoulders, big, pendulous ears, and upwardly-curving horns that can be huge. The breed originated in India, which is probably why it is able to tolerate hot, humid weather and pesky insects.

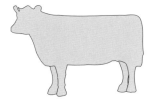

Charolais

Originating in France, these rugged, large-framed animals, with a white or creamy-white pigmented coat, like the heat but can also withstand reasonable cold. They are good at being herded and produce consistent quality beef, although for me it is not the best.

Dexter

An Irish breed, Dexters are small-bodied (tiny, really, in the land of big beasts), calm, and easy to look after. They are solid black, sometimes with a tiny flash of white on the face. While notoriously bad for milk, they give truly delicious beef. A well-grown, well-slaughtered, well-hung piece of Dexter beef will be sweet and smoky—one of my favorites.

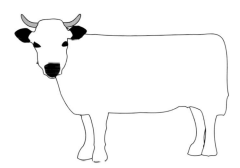

Chianina

The largest framed of all cattle breeds, the Chianina is usually short-haired, white to gray with black points, with long legs and well-defined muscling.

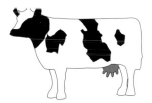

Holstein

The classic black and white dairy cow—the ones that graze away as we drive past, but which you suspect have a conversation once we have gone. The Holstein dominates the American milk production industry.

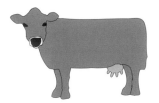

Jersey

This dairy cow ranges in color from light gray to dark fawn. It makes good cream and lots of milk, more per body weight than any other breed. The females are docile, the bulls anything but.

Lincoln Red

Native to the UK, females of this breed once made the milk for the great Stilton cheese. They are meat-producing beasts now, and have proved to be one of Britain's greatest exports as they are resistant to tsetse fly. They have reddish-brown coats but no horns.

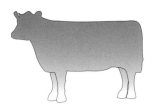

Limousin

Golden-red and sturdy, the Limousin is probably the most successful breed of commercial beef cattle, now often crossed with the Angus and the Shorthorn. The beef they yield is leaner than that from other breeds.

Texas Longhorn

These mighty beasts have impressively long horns and thick necks to carry that great weight. They are beautiful—a mix of black, gray, brown, and white, mottled. When slaughtered too early the meat is nowhere near what it should be. If the beast is left to grow and graze on grass—wow! What a piece of beef!

Polled Hereford

Polled Herefords are medium-framed animals with reddish-brown coats and large white faces. They look like they are wearing white socks, though they do have short, stumpy legs. The "polled" means they are naturally hornless.

Shorthorn

A legend among the beef-producing animals, the Shorthorn has a coat that ranges from white to brown but is broken up with rust-colored markings. Its horns are small, as the name suggests, and like the Longhorn, it needs a good three years to make great beef. It's not bad as dairy cattle either.

Santa Gertrudis

Rightly called America's first original beef breed, this is a cross between the Brahman and the Shorthorn. The beasts are a beautiful deep-red color, and are reared for both milk and beef.

Simmental

One of the oldest cattle breeds in the world, the Simmental is reared on all six continents, possibly because, compared with other breeds, it is thought to have the fastest rate of weight gain.

'BEEF CUTS'

Chuck

This has to be the most-used muscle in the whole beast, and as such it gives great lean, fibrous meat in huge pieces. If sliced very thinly and marinated, it can be grilled. It also works well for things like satay, as long as it is cut into thin, thin strips. I love a chuck blade roast left on the bone and braised, then stripped off and shredded—it has great flavor. Chuck also yields the best ground beef, with a high fat content for juicy hamburgers, and chunks for stew.

Rib

The upper middle part of an animal that walks on all fours will yield the tenderest, most prized pieces of meat for the mere fact that this is the only muscle that a quadruped does not use. In beef, the upper middle primal cuts are the rib and the short loin (below).

For a celebration, nothing beats an impressive standing rib roast, preferably dry-aged to insure that the flavor is at its best. The rib also yields tender, richly flavored steaks, such as the boneless rib steak (also known as spencer steak, delmonico steak, beauty steak, entrecote, and market steak) and bone-in rib-eye steaks, which are called cowboy steaks when the bone is frenched. I use the French name, *côte de boeuf*, for big bone-in rib-eye steaks.

Short Loin

One of the two most prized beef cuts (with rib), the short or strip loin lies along the middle back of the animal. Expensive steaks and roasts are cut from the short loin, and the tenderloin (fillet) starts here—it ends in the sirloin.

Of the approximately 680 pounds of meat and bone on a steer carcass, only 12 to 16 pounds is tenderloin. It is surrounded by a film of fat, most of which can simply be peeled away with the fingers, and then a silver skin that should be eased away with a very sharp knife.

The smaller, pointed end of the tenderloin is classically used for stroganoff and steak tartare. The thick center is used for chateaubriand, or simply as a roast (though it will need a little fat left in the creases should you wish to do that), as well as for steaks, such as filet mignon and tournedos (as in Rossini with truffle and foie gras), and for carpaccio.

The short loin yields club steaks (with the bone attached), New York strip steaks (without the bone), and porterhouse and T-bone steaks (both with bone and portions of the tenderloin), as well as bone-in or boneless strip loin roasts. All short loin roasts and steaks are succulent due to their marbling of fat and should never be cooked beyond medium rare.

Sirloin

The sirloin is the upper hip of the beast. There are three parts: the top sirloin, the end of the tenderloin, and the bottom sirloin (some of the bottom sirloin may be included in the knuckle or tip part of the round). Many beefers like myself prefer the full, rich flavor of sirloin steaks, rather than short loin or tenderloin steaks, even though sirloin may not be as tender. This cut also yields succulent roasts with a firm, satisfying texture and intense beefy flavor.

Round

Lean round is the entire upper part of the leg. It is divided into the knuckle, the top round, and the bottom round. Because the cuts from the round are lean and less tender than other cuts, they are normally braised or cooked by other moist, low-heat methods.

The knuckle (also called beef tip), which comes from the top of the round next to the sirloin, can be cut into roasts, steaks, and cubes for kabobs. If marinated, ball tip roasts can be dry-roasted and have good flavor.

Top round is the most tender cut from the round, but it is very lean and dense. While it can be roasted, it does well if pot-roasted or braised, because it can be dry if overcooked.

The bottom round muscle is well exercised, so cuts from this part of the round are tougher and have more connective tissue.

Brisket & Foreshank

Brisket comes from between the front legs. On a young beast the brisket will be flavorless and fatty; however, an older animal that has had plenty of time in the field will produce brisket that is a truly delicious delight. It is not a tender piece of meat, but the texture and flavor—wow! It is the cut of choice for Texas barbecue and makes the very best corned beef.

Those who know me well understand why I love beef shank. On or off the bone, it has to be the ultimate in braising and stewing meat. The muscles are wrapped around huge bones, which are filled with delicious marrow. The thing I really love, however, is the meat's structure.

As it cooks slowly and gently, the collagen that holds the muscle together and keeps it attached to the bone just melts away, leaving juicy meat and a delicious sticky sauce.

Veal shank comes from both the front and hind legs, and crosscut rounds of shank with a section of bone in the middle are osso buco.

Plate

In real terms, plate is the belly of the beast. Cuts from the plate have superb flavor.

Lean, coarse-grained skirt steak will absorb bold flavors beautifully when marinated. It is the authentic meat for fajitas, which take their name from the belt shape of the steak. Skirt steak is also sold coiled into a round shape, to be cooked as individual steaks.

Short ribs cut from the plate are fattier but meatier than those from the chuck and loin. With long, slow cooking by roasting or braising, they become lusciously tender.

Flank

The flank lies behind the plate on the underside of the animal. Although it is a little chewy, flank steak is ideal for marinating and then grilling. It is a very tasty steak for the money. The interestingly named London broil was originally a grilled marinated flank steak, although the term is nowadays applied to other steaks too. Flank also yields ground beef.

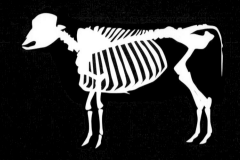

STOCKS SOUPS & GRAVY

Real stock is a great thing. As an apprentice I was taught to make a true beef and veal stock, which, I admit, needs time, patience, and a big pot. The great thing about making any stock is that once you've gotten all the flavor into the liquid, you can strain it, then put it back on the stove and boil it and boil it until it's a syrup. Culinarily this is called "glace de viande," or glaze of meat—effectively it's a bouillon cube. I freeze this like ice cubes and bring them out when making a sauce. I find the whole process satisfying but understand why some may think it's a drag. If you want to make a soup or sauce quickly, and need to cheat, there are cartons or cans of stock or bouillon available as well as concentrate in all sorts of packets and cubes. But be sure you buy a good one.

'BEEF STOCK'

Makes 5 quarts

5 lb. beef bones
4 large carrots, roughly chopped
4 large onions, roughly chopped
vegetable oil
2 heads garlic, halved
1 bunch celery, roughly chopped
2 large leeks, roughly chopped
a few bay leaves

Shank bones are ideal for this as their natural gelatin makes the stock especially sticky. Instead of all beef bones, you could use a mixture of half beef and half veal bones and add a pig's foot.

Heat the oven to 400°F. Put the bones in a large bowl or the sink and cover with cold water. Add a handful of salt and leave for 10 minutes—this will draw out the blood.

Throw the water away and put the bones in a large roasting pan with the carrots and onions. Sprinkle with a little oil and roast until brown (and I mean brown), about 40 minutes.

Pour everything from the roasting pan into a stockpot. Add the remaining ingredients, cover with water, and bring the stock to a rolling boil. Pour in about 2 cups cold water, which will set any fat as it rises to the surface. Adjust the heat so that the stock simmers very gently and start skimming the gray foam that will come to the surface. (As an apprentice we used to put our egg shells in the stock, because they would help collect all the muck.)

Keep the stock simmering for 8 hours, skimming as necessary. Strain the stock and let it cool overnight. Any remaining fat will settle on top and is easy to lift off and throw away, leaving you with a good clear, well-flavored stock.

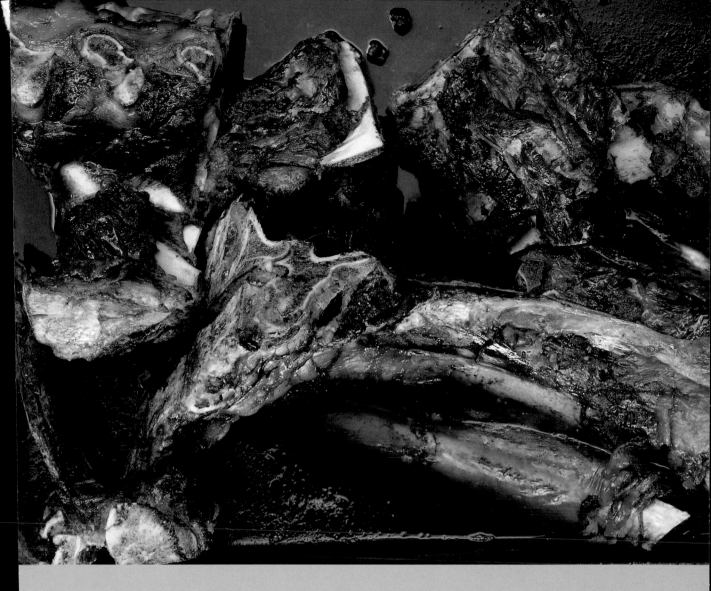

'BASIC VEAL STOCK 1993'

veal bones
beef bones
water
1 large "Gastro Mirepoix" of
   fresh vegetables (carrots,
   onions, leeks, celery)
herb stems (basil and parsley,
   can be found in pastry fridge)
5 heads garlic, cut in half

This is the veal stock recipe from Quaglino's and Mezzo, two restaurants in London where I once worked. We would use over 90 pounds of bones each night. The boilers would hold 40 gallons of liquid and the Bratt pan (a large pot that tilts to allow pouring) over 26 gallons. Stocks would simmer as we slept, then early in the morning they were strained and we would have access to good clear stock right away. Looking back, I love the regimental nature of this recipe, so I have included it as it stood in the kitchen. There's no need to make 40 gallons, of course, but this tasty stock is great for general home cooking too. You'll need about 6 pounds of bones and one head of garlic to make 3 quarts of stock.

Lightly brown bones in oven. Do not burn.

Place bones in boiler or Bratt pan.

Add water and bring to a boil, skimming frequently.

Simmer for 15 minutes, skimming frequently, and then add mirepoix, herbs, and garlic.

These stocks should be on at 1:00pm. These can be simmered until 11:30pm. They should then be left on low heat until 8:00am next morning. The stocks should then be passed off and put in tall pans to reduce.

Inform kitchen porters that the boiler and Bratt pan are ready for cleaning.

NB1: Do not boil stocks as they will go cloudy and greasy.
NB2: The Bratt pan must be cleaned by 7:45am to enable crustacea to cook their shellfish. Under no circumstances should the sauce section prevent crustacea from using the Bratt pan. It is used first and foremost for cooking off shellfish.

'FRENCH ONION SOUP WITH GRUYÈRE CROÛTE'

7 Tbs. butter
4 large onions, thinly sliced
salt and pepper
4 tsp. malt vinegar
4 tsp. brandy (optional)
2½ cups beef stock (recipe on page 22)
4 slices baguette
1½ cups grated Gruyère cheese

This is a meal rather than just a big bowl of soup. Onion soup is one of those great things that needs to be dripping off your chin, so don't try to be dainty with this soup—slurp and munch instead. Be careful with the bowls and the bread when they first come out of the oven—they will be super-hot. Cheat, if you wish, by toasting the bread and dropping it into the soup.

Heat the oven to 400°F. Melt the butter in a saucepan, add the onions with a generous grind of pepper and some salt, and cook slowly until golden, about 5 minutes. Add the vinegar and stir well—you will see the onions really getting brown. Keep the heat high and keep stirring. It will smell great.

When the onions are sticky and brown, pour in the brandy, if using. Strike a match and flame the pan, then pour in the stock immediately so you don't burn off all the booze—I like to taste it on the back of the throat. Bring to a boil, then reduce the heat so the soup simmers slowly for at least 20 minutes.

Meanwhile, put the sliced bread into the oven for a few minutes to crisp up.

Pour the soup into individual ovenproof bowls and float the bread on top so that it nearly covers the surface of the soup. Sprinkle the cheese over the bread, then carefully transfer the bowls to the oven. Bake until the cheese bubbles and turns golden brown, about 10 minutes.

The bowls are HOT, so take care when serving.

'CONSOMMÉ, POACHED EGG, AND TRUFFLE OIL'

1 carrot
1 celery rib
1 shallot
salt and pepper
10 oz. lean ground beef
2 egg whites
4 ice cubes, crushed
3¼ cups beef stock (recipe on page 22)

for serving
4 eggs
splash of vinegar
2 tsp. truffle oil
1–2 Tbs. minced fresh chives

This recipe needs great stock. It is one dish where you really should try to make your own.

Put the carrot, celery, shallot, and some salt and pepper in a food processor and pulse until the vegetables are finely chopped. Add the ground beef, egg whites, and ice, and pulse again.

Combine the stock and meat mixture in a large saucepan set over low heat. You want to heat the stock slowly so that the meat mixture floats to the top, creating a sort of raft. This will flavor the stock and make it beautifully clear.

Now increase the heat a little so that the liquid barely simmers—you do not want it to boil at all. Simmer for 30 minutes, then remove from the heat and let it sit while you poach the eggs. NEVER STIR OR THAT WILL BE THAT, AND YOU WILL BE EATING DRY GROUND BEEF SOUP—NOT GOOD.

Poach the eggs in a large saucepan with a little vinegar added to the water. Meanwhile, heat your serving bowls.

Strain the consommé gently—preferably through cheesecloth. It's most important that you do this slowly. Put a poached egg in the bottom of each bowl and ladle the consommé over. Sprinkle with the truffle oil and chopped chives, and serve.

If preferred, you can make the consommé in advance and store it in glass in the refrigerator for up to 5 days, or in the freezer for up to 6 months.

'TRUFFLE SOUP WITH PASTRY TOPS'

4 cups consommé (recipe on
  page 27)
1 large truffle, well brushed
1 egg, beaten
1 sheet puff pastry, about 7–8 oz.

This is a classic restaurant dish that looks fantastic when served in a lion's head bowl. The soup has to be warm or the puff pastry will melt into the bowls rather than rising in a majestic way. Make the consommé a day before serving.

Heat the oven to 400°F. Warm the consommé in a saucepan. Take your serving bowls and shave some truffle into each. Cover with the consommé.

Brush the egg around the rim of each bowl. Cut the pastry into circles slightly bigger than the top of the bowl. Lay the pastry over the bowls and press to seal.

Put the bowls on a baking sheet and place in the oven to bake for about 20 minutes. The pastry should puff up like a balloon as the soup heats. When done, the pastry should be crisp on top; the underside will be soggy from the steam of the soup.

Take the hot bowls carefully to the table. When your guests open the pastry lids, the room will fill with the heady scent of truffle.

'MUSHROOM SOUP WITH MUSHROOM TOAST'

1 ³/₄ lb. mixed cremino and
   portobello mushrooms, cut
   in chunks if large
6 Tbs. (³/₄ stick) butter
1 small onion, roughly chopped
1 celery rib, roughly chopped
2 leeks, roughly chopped
salt and pepper
³/₄ oz. dried porcini, crushed
   to a powder
2 garlic cloves, crushed
²/₃ cup peeled and chopped
   potato
3 fresh thyme sprigs
1 bay leaf
2 quarts beef stock (recipe on
   page 22)
scant 1 cup heavy cream

mushroom toasts
drizzle of olive oil
1 large shallot, diced
handful of chopped fresh
   flat-leaf parsley
6 slices sourdough or similar
   artisan-made bread
handful of grated Gruyère or
   Cheddar cheese

This soup is low in calories, but it has a true beefy-mushroom flavor from the dried mushrooms and beef stock. If you are going to use store-bought beef stock or beef bouillon, buy double. Then, before you start to make the soup, bring the stock to a boil and reduce it by half, to get a better, more concentrated flavor.

Set aside one-fifth of the fresh mushrooms for topping the toasts.

Melt half the butter in a large saucepan and cook the onion, celery, and leeks until soft but not colored. Add some salt and pepper, then the porcini powder and garlic. Cook for a minute or so. Add the larger batch of fresh mushrooms and cook, stirring, for a few minutes until they are soft and smell mushroomy. Add the potato, thyme, and bay, and stir until they are fragrant.

Pour in the stock, bring to a boil, and cook for 15 minutes. Discard the herbs, then purée the soup to the consistency you like, using a blender or food processor.

To make the toasts, heat the broiler. Season the reserved fresh mushrooms well with salt and pepper and drizzle with a little olive oil. Place them under the broiler and cook for 4–5 minutes on each side. Meanwhile, heat the rest of the butter in a pan and soften the shallot over medium heat. Chop the broiled mushrooms roughly and add to the shallot. Cook for 2 minutes, then add the chopped parsley and season with salt and pepper.

Toast the bread on one side only under the broiler. Turn the bread over and spoon the fried mushroom mixture onto the uncooked side so that all the juice is soaked up by the bread. Cover with the grated cheese and broil until bubbling.

Bring the soup back to a boil and add the cream. Taste and adjust the seasoning, if needed, then serve with the toasts.

'RICH BEEF & BARLEY BROTH'

2 lb. boneless beef shank

1 large onion

1 large carrot

1 turnip

1¾ cups beef stock (recipe on
  page 22)

1 heaped tsp. flaked sea salt

ground white pepper

1 Tbs. pearl barley

large handful of chopped
  fresh parsley

Cut the meat into 1-inch-square pieces and drop them into a bowl of cool water to soak for half an hour. This removes any excess blood that would make the soup bitter and cloudy; however, if you are using kosher beef you can skip this stage.

Meanwhile, peel the vegetables and cut them into pieces about the same size as the meat.

Put a heavy-based pot over medium heat and add the stock and vegetables. Drain the meat and add it to the pot with the salt and some white pepper. Bring to a simmer. Add the pearl barley, then reduce the heat a little so the liquid just simmers (the meat will get tough if you let it boil). Cook for 1½ hours. While the soup cooks, use a ladle to skim off any impurities that float to the surface. Alternatively, you can put the pot of soup in a 350°F oven and let it cook for 2 hours while you go and have a walk or something—I think that's a nicer way of making this.

Stir the parsley into the soup (the result is rather like a stew, not very brothy), just before serving it with lots of hot bread.

'ONION GRAVY'

Makes 2 cups

4 tsp. beef drippings or
    vegetable oil
4 lb. large white onions
salt and pepper
1 Tbs. malt vinegar
4 Tbs. ($\frac{1}{2}$ stick) butter
$\frac{1}{4}$ cup all-purpose flour
$1\frac{1}{4}$ cups beef stock (recipe on
    page 22)

When I roast beef at home, I keep the drippings (the fat from the meat left in the roasting pan) because I like to use it for other cooking—just like my grandma did. Beef drippings will deliver the very best flavor in this recipe, but you can always use vegetable oil if preferred. This recipe will serve at least six people (I like lots of gravy) and leftovers are easily used up— served with meatballs (page 231), or sausages, or stirred into sauce poivrade (page 217). You'll find my grandma's gravy recipe on page 153.

Place a good-sized saucepan over high heat and add the drippings or oil. Slice the onions and add them to the pan. Season with salt and pepper and stir until wilted.

Add the vinegar and continue to cook, stirring often, until the onions have some color, at least 10 minutes. Add the butter and stir until it has melted. Sprinkle in the flour and keep cooking and stirring for 5 minutes.

Pour in the stock and give a good stir, scraping the bottom of the pot to take off all the crust that has built up from the flour (this is full of flavor and will thicken the gravy). Bring to a boil and cook for 6–7 minutes, stirring constantly. Taste and adjust the seasoning as necessary before serving.

CARPACCIO

The great carpaccio is famously named after the Italian Renaissance painter Vittore Carpaccio, who loved to contrast red and white. Well, that's the story anyway. Many will argue that carpaccio should be simply raw beef tenderloin sliced very thinly and served with a sprinkle of olive oil, lemon juice, pepper, and salt. Delicious as that may be, we can be a little more exciting. Here you'll find some fantastic toppings for carpaccio, each of which creates a very special dish. The beef tenderloin you use for carpaccio should be fresh, fresh, fresh. Unlike most beef cuts, tenderloin benefits very little from dry-aging on the bone (with one exception—read on!). And aging shrinks it. It's an expensive cut, so you don't want any less of it. Another thing to remember: Don't freeze tenderloin, or it will turn to mush.

'BASIC RECIPE: CARPACCIO'

7–9 oz. center-cut beef
   tenderloin
good-quality olive oil
salt

If you prefer, you can use tenderloin tail, which is cheaper. You need about 2 ounces beef per person for an appetizer. Wrap the beef in plastic wrap and tighten each end like a sausage so that the beef has a neat shape. Refrigerate for an hour or so before slicing. Chill the serving plates in the refrigerator, too.

Just before you slice the beef, lay out the plates and put a drop or two of olive oil and a little salt on each one—this will give the beef a better depth of flavor and prevents it from sticking.

Trim off all the fat from the beef, then slice the meat as thinly as possible.

Lay four squares of plastic wrap on the work surface. Place an equal amount of sliced beef on each piece of plastic, positioning the slices so they do not overlap. Top with another sheet of plastic wrap and press down to seal.

Using a rolling pin, gently tap the beef so that it spreads out and becomes wafer-thin—if possible, about the same size as the plate you are going to serve it on.

Remove the top layer of plastic wrap and invert the carpaccio onto a plate. Peel off the other piece of wrap. Drizzle with a little olive oil and use your fingers to spread the oil all over the meat (this prevents it from changing color and drying out). Now, remember you're not a restaurant chef. A bit of artistic license is fine, but don't make the carpaccio looked too arranged—just sliced and plated.

Serve with any of the dressings or toppings you'll find on the following pages.

Classic Cream Dressing

Potatoes with Capers & Anchovies

Mozzarella, Beets, Fava Beans
& White Anchovies

Watercress, Gorgonzola
& Parmesan Dressing

Arugula, Lemon & Truffle Oil

Pan-Grilled Radicchio

Jalapeño, Mirin & Soy

Black Truffles

Classic Cream Dressing

1 large egg
1 egg yolk
1 Tbs. Dijon mustard
1 Tbs. shallot vinegar
1 garlic clove, crushed
7 fl. oz. vegetable oil
7 fl. oz. olive oil
6 oz. Parmesan cheese, grated (about 1½ cups)

Whisk the whole egg, yolk, mustard, vinegar, and garlic together in a large bowl until the mixture begins to thicken and turn pale. Slowly add the oils, whisking constantly, until well amalgamated. Add a little hot water if the mixture seems too thick. Stir in the grated cheese. Drizzle the dressing over the prepared plates of beef. Makes about 2 cups.

Potatoes with Capers & Anchovies

7 oz. fingerling or other small boiling potatoes,
   scrubbed
2 Tbs. olive oil
salt and pepper
½ Tbs. butter
2 tsp. capers
3 anchovy fillets preserved in oil, roughly chopped
juice of 1 lemon
a few fresh tarragon leaves, roughly chopped

Boil the potatoes for 10 minutes, then drain. Heat the oil in a frying pan. Add the potatoes and fry until colored and tender, 5–10 minutes, stirring often. Grind in a generous amount of pepper. Add the butter and, once it has melted, add the capers and anchovies and let them sizzle for a minute or so until the capers start to pop and turn crisp.

Take the pan off the heat and pour the lemon juice over. Add the tarragon and season to taste with salt and pepper. Let cool slightly while you prepare your four plates of carpaccio, then serve the beef with the seasoned potatoes.

Mozzarella, Beets, Fava Beans & White Anchovies

2 bunches baby beets, greens removed
4 oz. shelled fresh, young fava beans (scant 1 cup)
4 tsp. red wine vinegar
⅔ cup extra-virgin olive oil
flaked sea salt and black pepper
2 large balls buffalo mozzarella
20 white anchovies, drained
hot fresh bread

Cover the beets with water and boil for 12–15 minutes; let cool in the water. In another pan, boil the beans for 2 minutes; drain and refresh in a cold water bath to stop the beans from cooking.

Mix together the vinegar, half of the olive oil, and some salt and pepper. Scrape off the beet skins, cut them in half, and drop into the dressing. Tear the mozzarella into pieces and scatter over the carpaccio. Follow with the beans, beets, and anchovies. Sprinkle the cheese with a little salt. Drizzle the remaining oil over the plates. Serve with hot bread.

Watercress, Gorgonzola & Parmesan Dressing

1 egg yolk
2 tsp. vinegar
2 tsp. water
3 heaped Tbs. grated Parmesan cheese, plus
   shaved Parmesan for garnish
7 Tbs. vegetable oil
2 Tbs. olive oil
4 tsp. light cream
salt and black pepper
4 oz. Gorgonzola cheese
bouquet of watercress

Beat the egg yolk, vinegar, water, and grated Parmesan in a bowl until white. Slowly add the oils, then add the cream and stir well. Taste and season with salt and pepper.

Crumble the Gorgonzola cheese over the carpaccio. Top with the watercress and pour a generous tablespoon of dressing over each plate. Garnish with shaved Parmesan.

Arugula, Lemon & Truffle Oil

2 oz. arugula
2 tsp. good-quality olive oil
flaked sea salt and black pepper
1 lemon, plus 4 wedges for serving
2 oz. Parmesan shavings
2 tsp. truffle oil

In a bowl, dress the arugula with the olive oil, some pepper, and a few flakes of sea salt, mixing well. Add a little lemon juice to taste (it needs to be sharp but not enough to make you screw your eyes up). Scatter the dressed arugula over the plates of carpaccio, followed by the Parmesan shavings. Drizzle with the truffle oil. Grind some more pepper over and serve each plate with a wedge of lemon.

Pan-Grilled Radicchio

3 heads of radicchio, cut in wedges
olive oil
coarse sea salt and cracked pepper
small bunch of fresh marjoram, parsley, or basil
1 juicy lemon
handful of Parmesan shavings

Heat the oven to 400°F. Spread and separate the leaves of radicchio. Rub with a little olive oil and season with salt and pepper.

Heat a ridged cast-iron grill pan or broiler pan for 10 minutes over a high flame until very hot, so that when you add the radicchio, it sizzles. Pan-grill the radicchio for a minute on each side, then put it in a ceramic baking dish. Drizzle with more oil, add the herbs. and bake for 10 minutes.

Remove the baking dish from the oven, turn the radicchio over and squeeze some lemon juice over it. Turn the radicchio and squeeze the lemon again, then let cool. Serve with the carpaccio and Parmesan, drizzling the beef with the lovely juice left in the baking dish.

Jalapeño, Mirin & Soy

The famed Nobu is a chef who has been successful in fusing South American and Japanese cuisines in his restaurants. This carpaccio is inspired by them and the most glorious yellowfin tuna dish they serve in a similar way to this. You can buy little sachets of instant dashi and make it up with water.

8 tsp. mirin
4 tsp. sake
2 Tbs. dark soy sauce
4 Tbs. dashi broth
2 fresh jalapeños

Mix all the liquids together and leave to one side. Slice the jalapeños and lay them out over the carpaccio like every second number on a clock. Pour the dressing over the carpaccio and let it sit for 3 minutes before serving, with chopsticks.

Black Truffles

This has to be the easiest carpaccio, but also the most decadent and costly. Few of us will ever get the chance to buy a beautiful big truffle and have the money to shave it over some raw beef, but I had to include this as it is gorgeous to look at and has a wonderful aroma. This is the only time that I recommend using dry-aged tenderloin for the carpaccio and to spend money on some great olive oil.

extra-virgin olive oil
salt and pepper
1 large black truffle (as big as you can afford)

Rub a good quantity of oil over the top of the carpaccio and season well with salt and pepper.

Take the truffle in your right hand and a truffle slicer (look, if you can afford a truffle, you can afford a truffle slicer) in your left, and shave away to cover the plate with wafer-thin slices of truffle. Serve with a great big glass of oaky chardonnay.

'FENNEL, TOMATOES, & OREGANO IN FOIL'

2 large tomatoes
2 large fennel bulbs
1 lemon, halved
handful of fresh oregano or sage
1 tsp. salt
1 tsp. ground black pepper
4 Tbs. (½ stick) butter

This makes a good accompaniment for carpaccio, or with beef grilled over coals. If you're not lighting the grill, you can cook the foil parcels in a 400°F oven.

Take two large pieces of foil approximately 12 inches square and place them on the work surface. Cut the tomatoes and fennel into quarters and cut the lemon in half. Take the oregano (or sage) and pick off all the leaves.

Put four pieces of tomato and four of fennel on each piece of foil and fold up the sides. Squeeze half a lemon over each, then drop the lemon halves inside the foil. Sprinkle with the herbs and add ½ teaspoon each of salt and pepper to each parcel. Finally, divide the butter between the parcels and seal them.

Set the foil parcels on the grill and cook for about 30 minutes. Remove from the heat and let cool slightly. Open the foil parcels at the table and serve with the prepared carpaccio.

'ROAST TOMATO SALAD'

bunch of mixed fresh herb
　　sprigs, such as sage, rosemary,
　　thyme, and basil
⅓ cup flaked sea salt
10 plum or Roma tomatoes,
　　halved lengthwise
2 grape leaves
1 large preserved lemon, or
　　2 baby ones
2 handfuls of pitted olives,
　　preferably large purple ones
handful of fresh flat-leaf parsley,
　　roughly chopped
handful of fresh curly parsley,
　　roughly chopped

dressing
3 Tbs. olive oil
2 tsp. walnut oil
1 Tbs. balsamic vinegar
1 tsp. lemon juice
½ tsp. sugar
salt and pepper

When in season, plum-type tomatoes are sweet and full of juice. What this recipe does is condense their juice and concentrate the flavors. If you're cooking tomatoes this way, you may as well prepare a lot—it's great to have roast tomatoes in the refrigerator ready to eat with meat and fish. This salad is inspired by the Middle East, with its beautiful purple olives and pungent preserved lemons.

At least 4 hours ahead, roast the tomatoes: Heat the oven to 225°F. If you don't have a convection oven, wedge the door ajar with a wooden spoon, so you can get the air circulating inside.

Twist and crumple the bunch of mixed herbs in your hands to release their aromatic oils. Sprinkle half of them over a baking sheet with half the salt. Lay the tomatoes cut-side up on top of that, then scatter the rest of the herbs and salt over. Roast the tomatoes until crusty on the outside but still soft on the inside, about 3 hours. Remove and let cool.

While the tomatoes are roasting, lay the grape leaves on a rack set over a roasting pan and place in the oven. Dry them out for about 30 minutes. Remove and let cool, then cut the leaves into thin strips.

Cut the peel from the preserved lemon, discarding the flesh. Cut the peel into thin strips. In a large bowl, gently combine the roast tomatoes with the strips of grape leaves, preserved lemon peel, olives, and both types of parsley.

Mix together all the dressing ingredients and season with salt and pepper to taste. Serve the tomatoes and dressing over the top of the carpaccio.

'FRESH GOAT CHEESE & BEETS'

2 lb. beets (about 4), with greens
4 oz. fine green beans
1 Tbs. pine nuts
1 Tbs. red-wine vinegar
2 Tbs. extra-virgin olive oil
1 garlic clove, crushed
1 Tbs. capers, drained and
   coarsely chopped
½ tsp. cracked black pepper
bouquet of watercress
½ small red onion, finely sliced
7 oz. soft, fresh goat cheese

This sweet-and-sour combination works really well with carpaccio. If your beets don't have leaves, you can substitute baby spinach.

Trim the greens from the beets. Scrub the beets, and wash the greens thoroughly. Bring a large saucepan of water to a boil and add the beets, then reduce the heat and simmer, covered, until tender when pierced with the point of a knife, about 30 minutes. Drain and let cool before peeling and cutting into wedges.

Bring another saucepan of water to a boil. Add the beans and cook until just tender, about 3 minutes. Remove the beans with tongs (leave the saucepan of water on the heat) and plunge them into a bowl of cold water. Drain well.

Add the beet greens and stems to the boiling water and cook until tender, 3–5 minutes. Drain and plunge into a bowl of cold water, then let drain thoroughly.

To toast the pine nuts, put a heavy-based pan over high heat and, when it's very hot, remove from the heat and add the pine nuts. Toss them every 30 seconds or so; within about 4 minutes they will be nicely toasted. Remove from the pan and set aside to cool.

Put the vinegar, oil, garlic, capers, and pepper in a jar, cover, and shake well. Toss together the beets and beet greens, beans, watercress, onion, pine nuts, salt, pepper, and some dressing. Pile on top of the carpaccio. Crumble the goat cheese over the top and drizzle with the remaining dressing.

'JAPANESE STYLE WITH TOBIKO'

½ oz. dried wakame, or 2½ oz.
  fresh wakame
1 English cucumber
3 scallions
2 oz. enoki mushrooms
1 Tbs. chopped pickled ginger
handful of fresh cilantro
about 2 Tbs. tobiko
  (flying fish roe)

dressing
¼ cup dashi broth
¼ cup dark soy sauce
¼ cup tamari (sweet soy sauce)
¼ cup sake
¼ cup mirin
¼ cup sugar

The wakame used in this salad is lobe-leaf seaweed that can be bought salted or dried. Either way, it needs to be soaked before use, to get rid of the salt in fresh wakame or to rehydrate the dried version. If you can find wasabi-flavored tobiko, use it.

Soak the wakame in water for 20 minutes; rinse, then soak again for 5 minutes. Rinse the seaweed and squeeze it dry.

While the wakame is soaking, peel the cucumber and cut it into julienne. Slice the scallions across at an angle. Wipe the enoki mushrooms and trim the base of the stems. Combine the cucumber, scallions, enoki, pickled ginger, and cilantro in a bowl and add the prepared seaweed. Toss together gently.

Put all the dressing ingredients in a small bowl and stir until the sugar has dissolved. Mix half the dressing with the salad and let it sit for 5 minutes.

Drizzle a tablespoon or so of the remaining dressing over each plate of carpaccio. Put a pile of salad in the center of each and garnish with the tobiko.

'ONION RINGS & TOMATO RELISH'

onion rings (recipe on page 131)

tomato relish

1 tbsp. vegetable oil

2 tsp. ground cumin

1 tsp. ground coriander

1 tsp. ground turmeric

1 onion, finely chopped

1 garlic clove, crushed

14-oz. can crushed tomatoes

salt and pepper

You can make the tomato relish the day before serving. Heat a tablespoon of oil in a heavy-based pan. Add all the spices and fry for 1 minute, then add the onion and cook for a few more minutes, stirring constantly, until the onion becomes translucent. Add the garlic and cook for 1 minute longer. Add the crushed tomatoes and bring to a boil. Cook until thick, about 10 minutes. Season well with salt and pepper.

Cook the onion rings according to the recipe on page 131. The best tip I can give you is to peel the onion twice, by which I mean take off the skin and then the next layer, too. Big rings, little rings— cook them all. Whether you serve them with the carpaccio or not is another matter (I always eat them while I'm cooking). Also, always use caution when deep-frying. Never leave the pan unattended, insure that the handle is not protruding from the stovetop, and have a tight-fitting lid on hand so you can cover the pan quickly if the oil should burst into flames.

Lay your carpaccio out on plates. Place a stack of onion rings in the middle and a generous spoonful of tomato relish on the side.

'CAPONATA, OLIVE OIL, & POACHED EGG'

3 large eggplants
2 long shallots
4 large plum or Roma tomatoes
4 celery ribs
7 fl. oz. olive oil
2 tsp. large capers
⅓ cup golden raisins
¼ cup good-quality red-wine
   vinegar
salt and pepper
⅓ cup pine nuts
4 extra large eggs
malt vinegar for poaching
extra-virgin olive oil for serving
crusty bread

It's important that caponata has a real kick—the sweetness of the dried fruit needs to be offset with a good slug of red wine vinegar. Just as importantly, the texture has to be right: you want soggy eggplant, plump raisins, and crisp celery for a good caponata.

Remove the calyx from the eggplant (the green bit on top) and cut the flesh into chunks about the size of your thumb. Chop the shallots, tomatoes, and celery to roughly the same size.

Add the oil to a large, heavy-based saucepan or Dutch oven and set over medium heat. Add the eggplant and cook slowly, stirring often, until soft, about 15 minutes. Take out the eggplant with a slotted spoon; enough oil should be left to cook the shallots.

Put the shallots in the pan and reduce the heat to low. Gently cook the shallots until clear. Add the tomatoes and continue cooking slowly so they break down to a mush. Return the eggplant to the pan. Add the capers (with a little of their liquid), raisins, celery, and vinegar, and cook for 20 minutes or so. Season with salt and pepper and stir gently so the mixture doesn't break up too much. The whole thing should smell sweet and sour.

Meanwhile, put a heavy pan over high heat and let it get really hot (about 10 minutes). Remove from the heat, add the pine nuts to the pan, and let them toast in the residual heat, tossing every 30 seconds or so, for about 4 minutes. When nicely browned, remove and set aside.

Poach the eggs in a large pan of gently simmering water with a good amount of malt vinegar. Lift out with a slotted spoon and drain.

Pile the caponata on the carpaccio and top each serving with a poached egg. Finish with a drizzle of extra-virgin olive oil and serve with crusty bread.

SALADS & SNACKS

Summer days, lunch or dinner outside, and maybe brunch, too—the salad is a fitting little ensemble for any time. Great salads have a complex taste, but each flavor should be distinct, and there must be a mix of sweet and sour, whether that comes from the dressing or ingredients like green papaya and beets. Texture is paramount—there must be crunch as well as the soft ooze that comes from a great dressing or well-cooked meat. Both salads and snacks should be appetizing and tasty, but they must not fill you up. They need to leave a clean, crisp flavor lingering as a prelude to the greatness of the next course, or maybe just the next mouthful. I like to make a few dishes and set them out in the middle of the table; it's a great way to eat, and they encourage conversation simply by being passed around.

'COLD ROAST BEEF SALAD WITH HORSERADISH, BEETS, & WATERCRESS'

4-oz. bouquet of watercress, stripped of the big stems

10 oz. roast beef, thinly sliced

creamed horseradish (recipe on page 130)

8 preserved baby beets, each cut into 4 wedges

black pepper

olive oil

There are few classic combinations that work as well hot or cold as roast beef, watercress, and horseradish. This salad has been created to use up leftover roast beef, but it is just as good with a freshly cooked sirloin roast left to cool to room temperature.

Lay out four large serving plates and drop some watercress on each. Lay some thinly sliced beef over this and then some more watercress. Now drizzle the salad with the creamed horseradish. Add any remaining beef and scatter the beets over the top.

Finish with the last of the watercress and some more creamed horseradish, then add a generous grinding of black pepper and a splash of olive oil.

'QUICK & EASY THAI BEEF SALAD'

10 oz. trimmed boneless
  top sirloin
a little vegetable oil
1 cup bean sprouts
6 lime leaves, shredded
  (optional)
1 cup fresh Thai basil leaves
  (or ordinary basil)
½ cup fresh cilantro
3 fresh long, slim red chiles,
  seeds removed and cut into
  thin strips

dressing
juice of 2 limes
2 Tbs. vegetable oil
2½ Tbs. fish sauce
1 fresh long, slim red chile,
  finely diced

This is quick-quick-quick and very tasty—great Saturday lunch food, or it can be served as an appetizer. Depending on the type of chiles you use, you can make it medium-hot or very hot.

Cut the beef into thin strips about the length of your little finger. Heat a heavy-based pan over high heat. When it is very hot, mix the beef with a little vegetable oil and throw it into the pan. Let sizzle for a minute to get color, then turn and cook for another minute. Remove the meat from the pan and let cool a little.

Toss together the bean sprouts, herbs, and fine strips of chile.

In a separate bowl, stir together all the dressing ingredients. Pour the dressing over the warm beef, then add the herb salad. Toss well and serve immediately.

'LARP OF BEEF'

1 lb. ground beef

2 Tbs. fish sauce

6 Tbs. lime juice

8 red shallots, sliced

¼ cup fresh mint leaves

¼ cup fresh cilantro

¼ cup roasted sticky rice
   (recipe on page 58)

1 tsp. crushed red pepper flakes

for serving

1 fresh long, slim red chile,
   finely shredded

handful of fresh cilantro

endive leaves and/or betel leaves

This is a great salad. In Thailand, there would be lots of other things in here, like liver and lung, and the meat would not be cooked at all, but I didn't think that would appeal as much to non-Thais.

Put the beef in a wok or saucepan with a little salted water and simmer until cooked, about 3 minutes. Take the pan off the heat and let cool to room temperature, then drain off the excess water.

Just before you want to serve it, add the fish sauce, lime juice, shallots, mint, cilantro, roasted rice, and pepper flakes. Check that the flavor is hot, salty, and sour; add a few extra drops of lime juice, if necessary, to sharpen and define the flavor.

Sprinkle the shredded chile and cilantro over the top. Serve with endive leaves and/or betel leaves, using them as edible cups to hold the meat mixture.

'RICE NOODLE & BEEF SALAD WITH MINT & PEANUTS'

1 lb. boneless top sirloin

½ tsp. freshly ground pepper

1 tsp. toasted sesame oil

1 Tbs. sugar

2 Tbs. Thai fish sauce

7 oz. rice vermicelli

3 Thai shallots, finely sliced

3 garlic cloves, finely sliced

½ cup fresh mint leaves, chopped

⅓ cup fresh Thai basil leaves

⅓ cup fresh cilantro, chopped

1½ oz. yard-long beans, chopped (about ⅓ cup)

1 cup roasted peanuts, chopped

sauce

1 Tbs. rice vinegar

4 fresh small red chiles, chopped

⅔ cup sugar

2 garlic cloves, crushed

1 cup hot water

7 Tbs. Thai fish sauce

2½ Tbs. lime juice

1 small carrot, cut into julienne

A real crowd-pleaser, this is an interesting salad because the sauce is used to rehydrate the vermicelli, making them soft and at the same time pumping loads of flavor into what can be very boring noodles. Use more mint and chile if you like a bigger flavor.

Put a cast-iron ridged grill pan or broiler pan over a high heat and let it get really hot (about 10 minutes). Cut the beef into long, thin strips and season with the pepper and sesame oil. Lay the beef strips in the pan and do not touch them until they start to smoke. Then turn them over and leave to cook a minute longer.

Combine the sugar and fish sauce in a mixing bowl. Transfer the beef into the mixture and toss well (the fish sauce works in place of salt and gives great flavor). Let cool.

To make the sauce, heat the vinegar in a pan. Remove from the heat and add the chiles, sugar, garlic, and warm water, then the fish sauce, lime juice, and carrot julienne.

Put the rice vermicelli in a large bowl. Pour the sauce over it and let soak until the vermicelli is soft. Drop in the shallots, garlic, herbs, and yard-long beans, then add the beef and mix together. Sprinkle with the chopped nuts, toss, and serve.

'SPICED SALAD OF BRAISED BEEF WITH ROASTED RICE'

beef

1⅓ lb. boneless sirloin, fat removed, cut in chunks

1¼ cups fish sauce

8 cups coconut milk

3 thumb-sized pieces fresh ginger, roughly chopped

1 head galangal, roughly chopped (optional)

lemongrass strips, bruised

10 lime leaves (optional)

salad

handful of white sticky (glutinous) rice

2 green mangos, peeled and cut into julienne

3 Thai shallots, thinly sliced

2 handfuls of fresh cilantro

1 stalk lemongrass, peeled and sliced into thin rounds

large handful of fresh Thai basil

large handful of fresh mint leaves

¼ cup nam jim dressing (recipe on opposite page)

This is a complex salad even by my standards, but I have to include it as it has been one of my favorites for about 10 years. It's the way we often used up the trimmings of beef in the Mezzo kitchen.

The flavor is intense, but the best part is the texture—the meat is stringy but soft, crisp, and salty. With the heat of the chile and the sourness of the green mango, it is an inspired combination. Master this salad and you will find it hard ever to beat it.

You can multiply the recipe as many times as you like for a dinner party or feeding the masses. It is truly addictive, so make lots—you can store the meat in the refrigerator for up to a week.

Put the meat in a large bowl and cover with the fish sauce. Seal with plastic wrap and refrigerate overnight.

The next day, heat the oven to 325°F. Remove the beef from the fish sauce and put it in a large roasting pan with the coconut milk, ginger, galangal, lemongrass, and lime leaves. Put this in the oven to cook for 1 hour, then raise the temperature to 350°F and cook for 40 minutes longer.

Increase the oven temperature again, to 425°F, and cook for another 40 minutes to caramelize the mixture. It should turn golden brown and most of the coconut milk should have evaporated. It will look like the whole thing is burned, but it is not. It's just fabulously tasty.

Remove the roasting pan from the oven (leave the oven on) and put the meat into a bowl or dish to cool. Do not refrigerate—the beef is much better served at room temperature—although you can obviously refrigerate any leftovers for the next day.

Meanwhile, soak the rice for the dressing in a bowl of cold water for 10 minutes. Drain well, then spread it out on a baking sheet and roast in the 425°F oven, stirring often, until it is lightly browned and smells nutty. Transfer to a bowl and let cool, then grind to a coarse powder with a mortar and pestle.

To make the salad, shred the beef and put the mangos, shallots, cilantro, lemongrass, basil, and mint in a bowl, tearing any very large mint leaves into pieces. Add the dressing and toss gently. Serve the salad and beef together, sprinkling the roasted rice over the top like sesame seeds.

'NAM JIM'

2 fresh large red chiles
2 fresh small green chiles
¼ cup palm sugar
¼ cup fish sauce
¼ cup lime juice

This quick and easy dressing is perfect for all the Thai salads. Make it fresh every time you want to use it.

Dice all the chiles, then, using a pestle and mortar, crush them with the palm sugar. Add the fish sauce and lime juice to taste and use as soon as possible, within 6 hours.

'SEARED BEEF TENDERLOIN WITH THYME'

12 black peppercorns
½ Tbs. flaked sea salt
leaves from a few fresh
   thyme sprigs
7 oz. center-cut beef tenderloin
7 Tbs. extra-virgin olive oil
juice of 1 lemon, plus 4 wedges
   for serving
2 handfuls of mixed salad leaves
   and sprouted seeds
2 oz. Romano cheese

Grind the peppercorns and mix with the salt and thyme leaves. Rub the beef lightly with some of the olive oil, then rub the pepper mixture all over the beef. Heat a ridged cast-iron grill pan or broiler pan until very hot (about 10 minutes). Put the beef in the pan and sear on all sides, then remove from the pan and leave to cool.

Use a long, sharp knife to slice the beef as thinly as possible. Place the slices on a board and press them with the flat side of the knife blade to flatten each slice and make it bigger.

Cover the serving plates with the beef. Season with salt and pepper, then drizzle with half the lemon juice. Toss the salad leaves and sprouts with some olive oil and a little more lemon juice. Scatter the leaves over the beef, then shave the cheese on top. Drizzle with a little more olive oil and serve with the lemon wedges.

'SEARED SPICED TENDERLOIN'

1 tsp. ground fennel seed
1 tsp. ground coriander
1 tsp. ground allspice
1 tsp. ground black pepper
1 tsp. salt
½ tsp. crushed red pepper flakes
7 oz. center-cut beef tenderloin
vegetable oil
pineapple relish (recipe on
   opposite page)

Seared beef is like carpaccio—a very versatile little number, although it does need to be paired with strong flavors. Here, the crusty coating has fennel and chile mixed with coriander and plenty of black pepper.

Combine the ground spices, salt, and pepper flakes and spread them out on a plate. Heat a skillet or a very heavy frying pan until really hot (you shouldn't be able to hold your hand over it).

Roll the beef in the spice mix. Once this is done, you must sear it as quickly as possible. Pour a little oil into the pan and add the beef. Move it quickly so the spices do not burn, but let the beef brown. It takes about 20 seconds on each side and around 2 minutes in total.

Remove the beef from the pan. Wrap it up in plastic wrap, sealing the ends like a sausage, then chill. When ready to serve, slice the beef very thinly and serve it with pineapple relish.

'PINEAPPLE RELISH'

Makes about 1½ lb.

½ pineapple
3 fresh green chiles
1 cup vegetable oil
3 whole cloves
2 star anise
2 small cinnamon sticks
leaves from 2 sprigs of fresh
   curry leaf
½ cup sugar
salt

(a)

1 tsp. coriander seeds
1 tsp. fennel seeds
1 tsp. cumin seeds

(b)

10 dried chiles, soaked in warm
   water for 15 minutes, then
   drained
1 thumb-sized piece fresh young
   turmeric, peeled

(c)

8 small Thai shallots, chopped
5 garlic cloves

Making the pineapple relish is like being at school. Add (a) to (b) and it equals wow!

Grind (a), (b), and (c) separately until fine.

Remove the skin, eyes, and core of the pineapple and cut the flesh into bite-sized triangles. Cut the green chiles into ½-inch strips and set them aside with the pineapple.

Heat a frying pan and add the oil. When it is very hot, add (c) and stir for 1 minute. Then add (a) and (b), plus the cloves, star anise, and cinnamon. Stir well until the mixture is fragrant.

Add the pineapple, green chiles, curry leaves, sugar, and salt to taste. Reduce the heat and cook, stirring, until the pineapple pieces are soft. Let simmer for 1 hour, stirring occasionally. Do not add water during cooking as this will dilute the taste. Let cool before serving. You can store the relish in a jar in the refrigerator for up to a month.

'PAN-GRILLED BEEF WITH THAI FLAVORS IN RICE PAPER'

1 lb. beef skirt steak, trimmed
a little vegetable oil
½ cup bean sprouts
1 large carrot, shredded
handful of fresh cilantro
handful of torn fresh mint leaves
handful of fresh basil
nam jim dressing (recipe on
   page 59)
24–32 rice-paper wrappers

marinade

1 stalk lemongrass
1 garlic clove, minced
1 shallot, minced
1 fresh Thai chile, minced
1 tsp. fish sauce
1 tsp. lime juice
1 tsp. water
1 tsp. toasted sesame oil
2 tsp. toasted sesame seeds

This takes 2 days to make because the beef needs time to marinate. If you want to make it the same day, you can use a piece of boneless sirloin, although you will lose the intensity of flavor provided by the marinating.

Slice the beef into strips roughly the size of your finger, cutting the meat against the grain.

Using a mortar and pestle or a food processor, grind all the marinade ingredients together to make a paste. Coat the beef in the marinade and place in a non-plastic container. Cover and let marinate in the refrigerator for 2 days.

When ready to cook, heat a ridged cast-iron grill pan or broiler pan until very hot (about 10 minutes). Add a little oil and drop the marinated beef onto the pan. Cook it fast so that it is charred outside and a little pink in the middle. Remove from the heat and, using a really sharp knife, slice the meat into the thinnest strips you can.

Mix together the vegetables and herbs. Sprinkle with a little nam jim dressing and stir.

Work with one rice-paper wrapper at a time: Dip it into a dish of cool water for 30–60 seconds, then lay it on a dishtowel to absorb the excess water. Pile some of the vegetables and as much beef as you like down the middle, then roll up. (If the rolls are too big to fit in your mouth, you have put in too much filling!)

Serve with the remaining nam jim dressing as a dipping sauce.

'THAI SATAY WITH PEANUT SAUCE'

peanut sauce

3 Tbs. vegetable oil

1 shallot, minced

1 Tbs. Thai red curry paste

2 fresh small red chiles, seeds
  removed and minced

1 heaped cup freshly ground
  peanuts or chunky
  peanut butter

3 Tbs. soy sauce

large handful of chopped
  fresh cilantro

satay beef

1 lb. boneless sirloin steak

7 Tbs. light soy sauce

7 fl. oz. mirin

6 Tbs. miso paste

The main vegetable market in Bangkok is Phat Klong Talat, which opens at 4 am. Street sellers set up to provide the traders and customers with breakfast. As you approach the stalls the smell is intoxicating. The best satay I have ever eaten came off some metal roof guttering filled with hot charcoal and covered with wire. This recipe is inspired by those great market sellers who could feed me satay for breakfast any day. The sauce works just as well with fish or chicken.

Start with the peanut sauce. Heat the oil in a saucepan over medium heat. Add the shallot and fry gently for 3 minutes. Add the curry paste and chiles and cook, stirring constantly, until the paste is fragrant, about 5 minutes. Mix in the peanuts (or peanut butter) and scant 1 cup water, and bring to a boil, stirring well. Stir in the soy sauce, then remove from the heat and let cool. Once the sauce is cool, stir in the cilantro.

Meanwhile, soak 24 bamboo skewers in warm water for about an hour. This makes it easier to thread the meat and prevents the wood from burning while the meat cooks, especially over coals.

To make the satay, cut the beef into thin strips about 1½ inches long, ½ inch wide, and ¼ inch thick. In a bowl, mix together the soy sauce, mirin, and miso paste, then stir in the strips of meat. Let marinate for 20 minutes.

Thread the meat onto the skewers, insuring the maximum amount of meat will be exposed to the heat so that it cooks quickly and stays moist. Grill the satay, preferably over coals (otherwise, on a very hot, ridged cast-iron grill pan). Turn the sticks over every 30 seconds or so—a good satay will only take a couple of minutes to cook if the coals or pan are hot enough.

Serve the peanut sauce as a dipping sauce for the satay.

'FRAGRANT SATAY WITH PEANUT & COCONUT SAUCE'

Soak 20 bamboo skewers in warm water for an hour. Cut the meat into strips about the size of your little finger. Drop the meat into a bowl with the light soy sauce and sesame oil and leave for a while, preferably an hour. Remove the meat from the marinade, thread onto the skewers, and refrigerate.

Meanwhile, combine the coconut cream and red curry paste in a saucepan and cook for 5 minutes over low heat—the mixture should become fragrant as the spices cook. Add the sugar and a small shake of fish sauce and give it a good stir, then add the peanut butter.

1 lb. boneless beef rib (with a little fat in it)

3 Tbs. light soy sauce

1 tsp. toasted sesame oil

½ cup coconut cream

2 Tbs. red curry paste

3 Tbs. palm sugar or light brown sugar

a little fish sauce

½ heaped cup chunky peanut butter

14-oz. can coconut milk

a little vegetable oil

handful of chopped fresh cilantro

Bring the sauce to a boil. Add the coconut milk, then return to a boil and taste. It should be spicy but not too hot, and it should be thick—more like peanut custard sauce than oatmeal.

Grill the satay, preferably over coals (otherwise on a very hot ridged cast-iron grill pan or broiler pan): Sprinkle the satay with a little oil and place the ends that have no meat over the edge so you can turn the skewers easily. They need to cook fast—only a couple of minutes if the coals or pan are hot enough. Turn them every 30 seconds or so. The beef should have a slightly crisp exterior but be pink inside.

Serve with the peanut sauce on the side, sprinkled with cilantro.

'BEEF IN BLACK BEANS & CILANTRO'

10 oz. boneless top sirloin

2 garlic cloves

4 coriander roots or stems

1 knob fresh ginger, peeled

¼ cup vegetable oil

3 Tbs. dry sherry

1 tsp. toasted sesame oil

4 scallions, sliced, white and green separated

1–2 Tbs. black bean sauce

for serving

ho fun (rice noodles) or boiled rice

2 handfuls of fresh cilantro

Beef in black bean sauce is one of those Chinese classics that can sometimes be bland. In this version, a paste of garlic and ginger adds real depth of flavor.

Cut the beef as thinly as possible into long slices, then cut the slices into strips. They need to be long and thin so that when the beef is cooked it mounds like spaghetti with a sauce. Use a mortar and pestle to pound together the garlic, coriander roots or stems, and the ginger.

Heat a wok over medium heat and, when it is hot, pour in the oil. Add the garlic-ginger paste, stir, and cook for a minute—the flavors will really get up your nose and give off a strange bubblegum-like smell. Add the beef, increase the heat, and stir-fry for a minute. Add the sherry and sesame oil, and stir-fry until the beef is browned. Throw in the whites of the scallions and the black bean sauce, and stir-fry for 3 minutes longer.

Serve with noodles or rice, sprinkling the cilantro and the green parts of the scallions over the top.

'KOFTAS, PEPPERS AND TZATZIKI'

2 tsp. cumin seeds

2 Tbs. coriander seeds

1 lb. ground beef

juice of 2 lemons

large handful of fresh mint, chopped

⅓ cup pine nuts, toasted

salt and pepper

1 extra-large egg, lightly beaten

6 red bell peppers

olive oil

1 garlic clove, peeled

⅔ cup plain yogurt

I'm still an Australian at heart and reckon you can't beat cooking in the great outdoors with your mates and plenty of beer. All three of the recipes here can be served on their own, but work even better together. Serve with Turkish flatbread or warm naan.

Heat the oven to 425°F. Put a heavy-based pan without oil over high heat. Once it is hot, take it off the heat and add the cumin and coriander seeds. Let them toast without any further heat until they change color and release their fragrance, 2–3 minutes. Crush them with a pestle and mortar.

Put the beef into a bowl. Stir in half the lemon juice, 4 Tbs. of the chopped mint, the pine nuts, and crushed spices. Season well with salt and pepper, then bind the mixture with the egg. Make the koftas by shaping the mixture into 10 little balls; refrigerate for at least 30 minutes.

Put the peppers on a baking sheet, rub with a little olive oil, and roast until dark. Take out, drop into a big bowl, and cover with plastic wrap. Leave for 10 minutes, then peel off the skins. Discard the cores and seeds, and cut the flesh into hunks—quarters are good. Mix the juices left in the bowl with the remaining lemon juice. Season with salt and pepper and taste, then add a dash of olive oil, if needed. Drop the peeled peppers into this dressing. (They can be kept for 2 days in the refrigerator, so this can all be done well before serving.)

To make the tzatziki, use a pestle and mortar to crush the garlic to a paste with a little salt. Put the yogurt in a small bowl and stir in the garlic paste and remaining mint.

To cook the beef koftas, heat 3 tablespoons of olive oil in a frying pan until fairly hot. Fry the koftas, turning occasionally, until they are golden brown and cooked through, 6–7 minutes. Serve hot, with the peppers and tzatziki.

'ĆEVAPČIĆI'

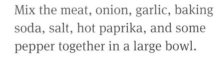

1½ lb. ground round
1 lb. ground lamb
12 oz. ground pork
2 Tbs. minced onion
3 garlic cloves, crushed
1 Tbs. baking soda
4 tsp. salt
2½ tsp. hot Hungarian paprika
black pepper
olive oil

The Vineyard in St. Kilda, Melbourne, Australia, was a restaurant that specialized in steak, and during my teenage years it was a huge inspiration to me. It was owned by the man who ran the local Yugoslavian soccer team. One of the dishes served as an appetizer at The Vineyard was ćevapčići (Yugoslavian sausage) with whole red bell peppers in their own juices. It was absolutely delicious. I was shown how to make ćevapčići in my fourth year as an apprentice. The main ingredients were ground lean beef, baking soda, hot paprika, and lots of garlic.

Mix the meat, onion, garlic, baking soda, salt, hot paprika, and some pepper together in a large bowl.

To form the ćevaps in the traditional way, moisten your hands with olive oil and shape the meat paste into sausages about 1 inch by 3 inches—you'll make 25 to 30 of them. Fry or, preferably, grill over hot coals and eat immediately.

'ANCHOVY, FONTINA, & MEAT SAUCE CALZONE'

dough

1 cup tepid water

3½ Tbs. olive oil

1 Tbs. honey

1 cake compressed fresh yeast

2 tsp. salt

2 cups all-purpose flour

filling

1½ cups grated Fontina cheese

4 oz. canned anchovies, drained

1 cup meat sauce (recipe on page 80)

I love these little parcels filled with cheese and meat and stuff—one is never enough.

Combine the tepid water, olive oil, honey, yeast, salt, and two pinches of flour in a saucepan and place over low heat. Cook until the mixture starts to bubble, about 5 minutes. Put the rest of the flour in a bowl and pour the liquid ingredients into it, mixing to form a dough. Knead until the dough is silky and strong—by hand this will take about 10 minutes (it's good exercise), or 5 minutes in a machine.

Cover with plastic wrap and leave somewhere warm. It will take about 40 minutes to double in size. Meanwhile, prepare the filling ingredients.

When the dough is ready, punch it down. Heat the oven to 500°F.

Roll the dough into a sausage shape, then cut it into 10 equal pieces. Roll out each one into a circle. Divide the cheese, anchovies, and meat sauce among them, piling the filling in the middle. Brush the edge of each dough circle with a little warm water, then fold one side over to give a half-moon shape and press to seal the edges.

Put the calzone on a baking sheet and bake until they are nicely colored, 10–15 minutes. Serve hot or at room temperature.

'OMELET WITH ASIAN GREENS, GINGERED BEEF & GARLIC'

filling
½ cup vegetable oil

2-inch piece fresh ginger, peeled and finely sliced

2 garlic cloves, crushed

8 oz. ground beef (about 1 cup)

8 oz. bok choy, leaves separated

8 oz. choy sum, leaves separated

2 tsp. toasted sesame oil

½ English cucumber, thinly sliced lengthwise

¼ cup fish sauce

omelet
5 large eggs, lightly beaten

fish sauce

¼ cup vegetable oil

Thai omelets (which are flavored egg pancakes filled with almost anything and usually deep-fried) are one of my favorite eats. This one is a two-stager because you have to make the filling. I know it sounds like a lot of work, but it is so good that it's worth it. In fact, you could charge people who come over for dinner and are served this omelet.

Start with the filling. Heat the oil in a wok over high heat, add the ginger and garlic, and cook for 1 minute. Add the beef and fry until browned but not dry, about 2 minutes. Add the bok choy and choy sum and toss until wilted, 3–4 minutes. Add the sesame oil and cucumber and cook for 3 minutes longer, stirring well. Remove from the heat, stir in the fish sauce, and set aside.

To make the omelet, lightly beat the eggs together in a bowl and season with a little fish sauce. Heat a clean wok over medium heat and add the oil, tilting the wok to coat it evenly. Pour in the eggs and roll around until the surface of the pan is covered, using the back of a spoon to spread the egg evenly. Once a skin has formed, let the omelet cook, still tilting the wok and smoothing, for 3–4 minutes, then lift the omelet out of the pan and place it on a clean dishtowel. At this stage the top of the omelet will still be a bit liquid, but it will continue cooking as it cools.

Lay the filling across the omelet and, using the dishtowel, lift one edge over the filling. Continue rolling the omelet as though you were making a jelly roll, so that the filling is securely enclosed. Cut the omelet roll across at an angle into four pieces and place them on serving plates. Serve immediately, with extra fish sauce for seasoning.

Tip Ideally, finely slice the cucumber using a mandoline (take great care if your machine doesn't protect your fingers as you cut). If you don't have a mandoline, you can use a vegetable peeler to cut the cucumber into thin strips.

'KOBEBA WITH GROUND RICE'

shell
8 oz. ground round (about 1 cup)
1¾ cups white rice flour
salt and pepper
about 6 Tbs. water

filling
12 oz. ground chuck (about
  1½ cups)
1 medium onion, grated
½ tsp. ground allspice
1 tsp. ground cinnamon

Like most Australians, I grew up with a mix of culinary influences. Foreign recipes, such as these traditional Mediterranean dumplings, filtered down to us from food in restaurants. It's important that the meat for the shell be very lean, or the dumplings could fall apart.

To make the shell, put the meat, rice flour, and ½ teaspoon salt into a food processor and pulse thoroughly. Add just enough water to produce a soft, dryish paste that holds together well.

Next, prepare the filling by working all the filling ingredients together by hand, with some salt and pepper, until a paste forms.

While making the dumplings, some people like to keep their hands wet so that the paste does not stick; other people flour their hands; and some oil them. For each dumpling, take a lump of the ground rice and meat paste, a little smaller than a walnut, and roll it into a ball. Make a dent in the middle of the dumpling with your finger, then pinch the sides and lift them up as though you were shaping a pot, making the shell as thin as possible. Stuff with 1 teaspoon of filling, then bring the sides of the shell up over the filling, pinching the edges together to close the dumplings. Roll lightly into a ball.

You can deep-fry or roast the kobeba in oil before poaching them, to give them a golden color and make them firm. I simply poach mine in beef stock or stew for 25 minutes.

Variations There are many ways you can change the flavoring of the filling, such as adding minced celery leaves or flat-leaf parsley. In Iraq, the filling will contain parsley or celery leaves, plus ½ teaspoon ground cardamom or 1 teaspoon pulverized dried limes, while in Calcutta, India, the filling is normally flavored with ginger, garlic, turmeric, and chopped cilantro.

'PELMENI'

dumpling dough
⅓ cup milk or water
1 egg
salt
2⅓ cups all-purpose flour

filling
3 oz. beef tenderloin or sirloin
   trimmings
2 small onions
1 garlic clove, crushed
salt
5 drops olive oil
handful of chopped fresh
   parsley

for serving
⅔ cup sour cream
large handful of fresh dill,
   roughly torn

My uncle's mother, Nanna Hinki, taught me to make these Russian dumplings when I was about eight. The filling needs to be smooth. You must mince the beef and the onions very, very finely so that they are almost a paste. The mixture should be sandy when cooked, at which point the oil is beaten into it.

Put the milk or water in a saucepan and bring to a boil, then add the egg and a pinch of salt and mix them together. Pour this mixture into the flour and stir to form a dough. Set aside to rest for about 40 minutes.

Finely mince the beef trimmings with a knife, then finely mince the onions. Make a smooth paste of the garlic with ½ teaspoon of salt. Now mix all the filling ingredients together in a large bowl and beat it and beat it and beat it into as fine a paste as you can.

Roll out the dough until it is about 1/16 inch thick. With a 2½-inch round cookie cutter or glass, cut out disks. This should make around 24 disks. Place a little ball of the filling paste in the center of each disk, then fold the dough over to make half-moons. Take the corners of each half-moon, curl them around your finger, and pinch together to seal—as though you were making tortellini or fortune cookies.

Drop the dumplings gently into a pan of slightly salty boiling water. Wait until the water boils again, then reduce the heat a bit and simmer for 7–10 minutes. When the pelmeni rise to the top, they are ready to be taken out with a slotted spoon. Remember to let the water drain away before you put them onto the plate.

To serve, toss with the sour cream and fresh dill.

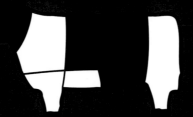

PASTA & RICE

The meat sauce recipes here make lots, so you'll have leftovers ready to put in the freezer. Cooking enough for more than one meal is something I think we should all be doing, rather than worrying about preparing quick dishes every day. Bolognese sauce is a godsend to anyone who has kids. I reckon more of it is eaten in my house than any other single dish. It goes on spaghetti, on toast, in toasted sandwiches, in cannelloni, under mashed potatoes, and into Jessie's (my wife's) famous and very, very good lasagne. For my ragù, you need ground beef with a good blend of fat and lean meat. The best formula will be something like 25 to 30 percent fat—yes, truly that much!—otherwise the sauce will not be moist. Most ground beef cooks quickly, and without enough fat it will turn grainy and sandy.

'MEAT SAUCE'

Makes about 2 quarts

2 lb. boneless beef shank and/or
   skirt steak, or beef cheek, cut
   into hand-sized chunks

salt and pepper

2 carrots

2 leeks

2 celery ribs

2 bay leaves

small bunch of fresh flat-leaf
   parsley, plus extra chopped
   parsley for serving

small bunch of fresh sage

about 6 Tbs. olive oil

8 oz. thickly sliced bacon, cut
   into large chunks

28-oz. can crushed tomatoes

1½ cups red wine

I like this sauce to be really sticky and thick. Using two forks to pull the meat apart is a classic technique: just dig in and pull—it works wonders.

Heat the oven to 375°F. Season the beef really well. Tie the carrots, leek, celery, and herbs together tightly in a bundle.

Heat the olive oil in a Dutch oven. Add the bacon and cook for 2 minutes, then add the beef. Wait until the chunks are well browned on the underside, then turn them over and cook for 10 minutes longer, making sure to turn the bacon, too (if it seems to be browning too quickly, you can always take it out and return it to the sauce at the next step).

Add the bundle of vegetables and herbs. Pour in the tomatoes and wine and bring to a boil. Let it bubble for about 10 minutes, scraping the bits of meat from the bottom of the pan.

Pour in 4 cups or so of water, enough so that it almost covers the meat. Put the lid on the pot and transfer to the oven to continue cooking for 1 hour. Take the lid off and give the sauce a good stir, then put it back in the oven to cook for another hour so that much of the liquid can evaporate. Remove the pot from the oven and let the sauce cool for half an hour or so.

Shred the meat well, using two forks to pull it apart. Chop the vegetables finely, discarding the herbs. Return the meat and vegetables to the pot. If the sauce is soupy, bring it to a boil to get rid of some of the liquid, but remember that this will be served with pasta or bread so it shouldn't be dry. Taste and adjust the seasoning as necessary. (At this point you could let some of the sauce cool and store it in resealable bags in the freezer.)

Fold a lot of chopped parsley through the sauce just before serving so that the parsley stays nice and green.

1 lb. ground round
olive oil
5 oz. chicken livers
1 large or 2 medium onions,
   chopped
4 garlic cloves, crushed
28-oz. can crushed tomatoes
a large squirt of tomato paste
2 beef bouillon cubes
generous handful of chopped
   fresh mixed herbs
most of a bottle of decent red
   wine, preferably Merlot
salt and pepper
1 glass amontillado sherry
freshly cooked spaghetti
freshly grated Parmesan cheese

For many years I worked on a morning TV program with Richard Madley and Judy Finnegan. They always boasted that their spaghetti bolognese recipe was by far the best. Well, time for you to judge! I have to say it's pretty good. I have eaten it a few times—better when made by Judy than by Richard!

Brown the beef in a large, deep frying pan with a little olive oil.

Ditto the chicken livers.

Put the meat to one side and place the onion in the pan.

Stir on medium heat until soft.

Stir in the crushed garlic. Do not brown it.

Add the beef, chicken livers, canned tomatoes, tomato paste, bouillon cubes, herbs, and wine.

Bring to a boil, stirring occasionally, then reduce to simmer.

Simmer for 1½ hours, stirring occasionally. If it looks as though it may be drying out and needs extra moisture during this time, add more wine or water.

Season with salt and pepper to taste and add sherry.

Serve 5 minutes later on a bed of hot spaghetti, with freshly grated Parmesan.

'MY MEAT RAGÙ'

2 lb. ground chuck

1 cup red wine

¼ cup vegetable or olive oil

2 large onions, diced

2 garlic cloves, crushed

salt and pepper

3 bay leaves

a shake of dried herbs, such as
    oregano or thyme, but not a lot

3 cans (14 oz. each) plum
    tomatoes

1 heaped Tbs. tomato paste

Someone, somewhere will say this is wrong, but this is how I do it! I learned to make this at age eight, from an Italian. A good ragù needs fat to keep it moist and full flavored, so be sure your ground beef isn't too lean. Make lots and store in the freezer for a rainy day.

Take the meat and massage the red wine into it so that the beef absorbs it. Heat a big, heavy pan. Add the oil and onions and cook gently (or sweat) until the onions are translucent. Add the garlic, a good amount of ground pepper, and a teaspoon of salt. Stir and stir until the garlic starts to give off a fragrant aroma.

Add the meat and herbs, and continue cooking and stirring for a few minutes until the meat starts to get a little color. Add the canned tomatoes and tomato paste and bring to a boil. Turn the heat down to a simmer and cook for 2 hours, stirring every half hour or so. Taste and adjust the seasoning as necessary, then serve with any pasta or gnocchi (recipes on pages 85–87).

'GNOCCHI ALLA ROMANA'

2 cups milk

1 garlic clove, crushed

salt and pepper

1⅓ cups fine semolina

1 cup freshly grated Parmesan
   cheese

1 cup grated Romano cheese

2 egg yolks

about ⅔ cup butter

oil for greasing

2 balls mozzarella cheese

meat sauce, bolognese, or ragù
   (recipes on pages 80–82)

handful of chopped fresh sage

Here is a recipe for semolina gnocchi; a potato version follows on the next page. The two are interchangeable and really delicious. Gnocchi alla Romana are usually baked in little dishes with meat sauce spooned over.

In a large saucepan, heat the milk to a scalding point with the garlic and some black pepper. Add the semolina and cook, stirring, until it thickens—it should be the same consistency as cornmeal mush. Take the pan from the heat and stir in the cheeses, really beating the mixture with a wooden spoon to get some air into it. When the mixture has cooled a little, beat in the egg yolks, about one-third of the butter, and season with a little salt and pepper.

Lightly oil a rimmed baking sheet and pour the semolina onto it so it's about the thickness of your finger. Let cool, then refrigerate for a few hours or overnight.

When the semolina has set, heat the oven to 425°F. Using a round cookie cutter or a large glass, cut it into disks. Butter the inside of 10 individual baking dishes (or one large dish) really well. Lay the semolina disks in the dish(es). Rub the tops with some more butter and bake for 10 minutes. The gnocchi should puff up and turn golden.

Take the dishes from the oven. Now, you can roughly tear up the mozzarella, scatter it over the gnocchi, and bake for 5 minutes until the cheese melts, then serve with your meat sauce. Or, you can spoon the meat sauce over the gnocchi, then cover with the mozzarella and bake for 5 minutes. Sprinkle with chopped sage before serving.

'POTATO GNOCCHI'

2 lb. russet or other dry, mealy
    potatoes
3 ⅓ cups all-purpose flour
salt
butter
meat sauce, bolognese, or ragù
    (recipes on pages 80–82)
freshly grated Parmesan or
    Fontina cheese

Peel the potatoes and cook them in a small amount of boiling water. Drain off all the water, then cover the top of the pot with a dishtowel and place the lid on the pot—this will help absorb the steam so the mashed potato will be fluffy. After 5 minutes, take off the lid and the towel and mash, mash, mash.

Pour the mashed potato onto a chopping board, add the flour and some salt, and knead to a dough while warm. It is ready when the dough comes away from your hands like Play Doh®.

Roll the dough into a sausage shape ¾ inch wide and as long as you can. Cut it into 1½-inch-long lozenges or pieces, or little sausages, or whatever you want to call them. Roll each one over the back of a fork to get some grooves in it.

Bring a big pot of water to a boil and drop in the gnocchi a handful at a time. They should float to the surface and then simmer (if they boil they will break up) for 3 minutes. Lift them out of the water with a slotted spoon and drop them into a bowl with some olive oil. You can do this the day before serving; if so, store in a covered container in the fridge once cooled off, and cover and reheat in the microwave as needed.

Arrange the gnocchi in a buttered dish and pour some meat sauce over them. Sprinkle with grated Parmesan or Fontina cheese and bake for 10 minutes.

'PASTA'

4 cups type "oo" (*doppio zero*)
  pasta flour, plus extra for
  dusting
salt
4 whole eggs, plus 3 egg yolks
1 Tbs. olive oil

I know there is plenty of great pasta on the market, and lots of people think making their own at home is too difficult, but it is very satisfying once you know the basics. And it allows you to make all sorts of parcels and shapes with whatever fillings you like. Use Italian "oo," or "doppio zero," flour, if possible. The recipe here makes enough dough for four to six good-sized ravioli for four people.

Put the flour and a pinch of salt into a food processor. Add half the eggs and half the extra yolks and mix until incorporated. Add the oil and mix again.

Beat together the rest of the eggs and yolks and add to the processor a little at a time. Stop and feel the texture of the mixture regularly. When it is ready, it will be like large, loose bread crumbs that will hold together as dough if you squeeze them between your fingertips. You may not need to use all the eggs, or you may need to add a little more.

Transfer the mixture onto a floured work surface and push it together, then knead until it forms a dough. Wrap in plastic wrap and let rest in the fridge for several hours before use. Roll out with a pasta machine following the manufacturer's instructions and cut into the desired shape.

'OXTAIL RAVIOLI WITH SOY & GINGER BROTH'

oxtail

1 large oxtail, cut in chunks

salt and pepper

about ½ cup all-purpose flour

¼ cup vegetable oil

1 large carrot, peeled and diced

1 onion, diced

½ celery rib, diced

1 garlic clove, crushed

1 knob galangal or fresh ginger, peeled and crushed

4 Tbs. (½ stick) butter

7 Tbs. port wine

1 cup red wine

about 1¾ cups beef stock (recipe on page 22)

2 Tbs. dark soy sauce

2 tsp. fish sauce

1 star anise

pasta

fresh pasta dough (recipe on page 87)

1 egg, beaten

salt

splash of olive oil

This recipe is seriously cheffy and I know that many of you will not want to make it, but the braised oxtail is gorgeous—it could simply be tossed with a few noodles and people would love it. However, if you do make the ravioli, it will be fun, and it's a good dish for getting the kids involved. The broth is also good served over noodles with some shredded vegetables and scallions, and maybe an egg.

Take a big Dutch oven and place it over high heat. Turn the oven on to 350°F. Trim the excess fat from the oxtail. Season it well with salt and pepper, then roll it in the flour. Heat the vegetable oil in the pot and fry the oxtail until well browned all over.

Take the meat out and set aside. Add the vegetables, garlic, and galangal or ginger to the pot, plus the butter, and cook until the vegetables are well browned, stirring all the time to scrape up the brown bits from the bottom of the pot. Pour in the port and boil until half the liquid has evaporated, then add the wine and do the same again.

Drop the oxtail back into the pot and stir quickly to coat with the sauce. In a large bowl, combine the stock, soy sauce, fish sauce, and star anise and pour this mixture over the oxtail (there should be enough liquid to cover; if not, add more stock). Stir well, then cover and transfer the pot to the oven. Cook for 1½ hours. Take the lid off and cook for 1 hour longer.

When the meat is done, lift the oxtail from the sauce and strip the meat from it. Strain the sauce, setting the vegetables aside and returning the sauce to the pot. Bring to a boil and keep boiling to reduce the sauce to a sticky syrup. In a bowl, mash the meat, then stir in the vegetables and a little sauce to give a stiff mixture that can be used to fill ravioli or tortellini.

Working in batches as necessary, put the pasta dough through a pasta machine, or use a rolling pin, to roll it out to paper-thin sheets. Work as quickly as you can, because the more the pasta dries out, the more it will lose its elasticity; while you are rolling each batch, keep the remainder moist by covering it with plastic wrap. Cut the dough into disks about 3 inches in diameter. Keep them wrapped in plastic wrap and set aside in a cool place until you are ready to fill them.

Lay half the disks on the worktop. Place a little of the meat mixture in the center of each disk and brush the edges with egg. Lay the remaining pasta disks over the top and pinch well all around the edges to seal.

To make the broth, put all the ingredients in a large pot, bring to a boil, and cook for 3 minutes. Remove from the heat and let infuse in a warm place until you are ready to serve.

Bring a large pot of salted water to a rolling boil, adding a drop of olive oil. If you don't have a large pasta pot, it is better to cook the ravioli in batches in separate pans. Add the ravioli. They will gradually float to the surface and will be ready 2 minutes after that (so about 4 minutes of cooking in all).

Meanwhile, strain the broth, discarding the solids, and reheat it. Do not let it come to a boil again or it will turn bitter. Drain the ravioli well and place one in each serving bowl. Sprinkle in some scallions and chiles, then ladle the broth over and serve.

broth

1³/₄ cups beef stock

1 tsp. fish sauce

1 knob fresh ginger, crushed

2 star anise

3 coriander roots or a handful of coriander leaves

1 Tbs. dark soy sauce

for garnish

2 scallions, sliced diagonally

2 fresh red chiles, sliced diagonally and seeds removed, if desired

Variation: Veal & Spinach Meatballs
Take about 14 oz. spinach leaves and wilt
them in a saucepan, with only the water
that's left clinging to them after washing.
Drain well and, once cool, squeeze the excess
water out with your hands so the spinach is
really dry. Put it in a food processor with
1 cup ground veal, 2 slices of bread that you
have softened in a little water and squeezed
dry, 2 eggs, some salt and pepper, and ½ tsp.
grated nutmeg. Blend to a paste. Shape the
mixture into balls, then roll them in flour
and fry in vegetable oil, turning until brown
on all sides.

'SPAGHETTI AND MEATBALLS'

²/₃ cup olive oil
2 large onions, finely chopped
salt and pepper
3 cups fresh bread crumbs
2 lb. ground beef
handful of chopped fresh
    parsley, or other herbs
1 cup red wine
6 large fresh tomatoes, chopped
28-oz. can crushed tomatoes
1 lb. dried spaghetti
freshly grated Parmesan cheese

This is a dish that should really be served out of the big cooking pot on the table. It needs to slop, drip, and splatter. The spaghetti has to be piping hot and soaked with sauce, then sprinkled with freshly grated Parmesan. A 1-pound package of spaghetti will be fine for four to six people as long as you have plenty of meatballs—everybody loves meatballs, so make lots.

Put the olive oil in a Dutch oven. Add the onions, plenty of black pepper, and some salt. Turn the heat to medium and cook the onions slowly until soft, but not colored. Remove from the heat.

Put 1 cup water in a large bowl. Add the bread crumbs and half the cooked onions, lifting them out of the pot with a slotted spoon. Lift out the rest of the onions, leaving as much oil as possible in the pot, and set them aside for the sauce.

Add the beef and chopped parsley to the crumbs. Season well with salt and pepper, mix until the whole thing becomes a paste, then shape into balls about the size of a Ping-Pong® ball.

Put the Dutch oven back over high heat, add the meatballs, and cook until browned, about 10 minutes. Gently turn them and continue browning. Take them out and set aside. Add the reserved cooked onions to the pot along with the wine. As it boils, scrape the brown bits from the bottom of the pot.

Add the fresh tomatoes and stir over high heat until they start to break down. Add the canned tomatoes and half the can of water. Bring to a boil and cook for 5 minutes. Put the meatballs back in the pot and return to a boil, then simmer for 15 minutes.

Meanwhile, cook and drain the spaghetti according to the package directions. I like to put everything together in the pot for serving, but many don't, so it's your choice.

'RISOTTO WITH GREEN GARLIC'

3 Tbs. butter

1 Tbs. olive oil

2 small shallots, diced

4 garlic cloves, crushed

about 4 cups beef stock

2 cups arborio rice

1 cup freshly grated Parmesan
cheese

large handful of green garlic
leaves, roughly torn

Here is a basic recipe to which you can add whatever you like—the rule is that ingredients that need to cook go in at the beginning, while herbs, leaves, and cooked ingredients are added at the end. Green garlic, which is young garlic that has not started to form cloves, is around for a short period only in the spring (look for it in farmer's markets and specialty food markets). If you can't get green garlic, try a mix of soft herbs, such as sage, basil, chives, and chervil.

Heat 1 tablespoon butter and the oil in a large, heavy-bottomed pan. Add the shallots and cook until just translucent, then add the garlic and cook for 3–4 minutes longer. Put the stock in a separate saucepan and bring it to a boil. Add the rice to the onions and stir around for a couple of minutes to coat the grains and stop them sticking together.

Your pot of boiling stock should be at the ready. It is important that the stock and rice are at a similar temperature, so that the heat doesn't fall when you add the stock to the pan. If it does, the rice may not rehydrate properly, which will result in it being cooked on the outside while remaining quite hard inside. Add a couple of ladles of stock and stir around until all the liquid is taken up and the rice can be scraped from the bottom of the pan.

Keep adding stock, stirring and scraping all the time, to avoid sticking. After about 15–20 minutes the grains will be tender but still firm to the bite and the risotto will be creamy and moist. Add the Parmesan and the remaining butter, and whip with a wooden spoon to put more air into the now-creamy rice. Throw in the torn green garlic leaves and serve immediately.

'WILD MUSHROOM & TRUFFLE RISOTTO'

1¾ cups beef stock (recipe on page 22)

4 oz. portobello mushrooms, sliced

¼ cup olive oil

2 shallots, diced

1 garlic clove, crushed to a paste

4 oz. wild mushrooms, cleaned and trimmed

salt and pepper

scant 1 cup Vialone Nano rice

scant ½ cup freshly grated Parmesan cheese

1½ Tbs. butter, diced

handful of chopped fresh parsley

1 small truffle, scrubbed

4 tsp. truffle oil

This is good hearty food that goes down well with most generations on most occasions.

Bring the stock to a boil in a large saucepan, then remove from the heat, drop in the portobello mushrooms, and stir.

In another wide saucepan, heat the oil and fry the shallots slowly, without letting them brown. When they look softish, add the garlic (it will burn if you put it in at the same time as the shallots). Drop in the wild mushrooms, season with a tiny amount of salt but lots of black pepper, and cook, stirring, for 1 minute. Remove the mushroom mixture from the pan, leaving behind as much oil as possible, and set aside.

Add the rice to the pan and stir quickly in one direction only, keeping the heat high. The rice will take up the oil. Although this is not a difficult dish, it's worth being patient. Add a ladle of stock and mushrooms into the pan of rice. Stir until all the stock has been absorbed, then add another ladle of stock and stir again. Keep going until all the stock is used or the rice is cooked, whichever happens first. For me the rice should be cooked but not mushy, and the consistency sloppy but not soupy.

Add the cooked wild mushrooms, the cheese, and butter and stir. Let the risotto rest for a couple of minutes, then serve, sprinkled with chopped parsley, shaved truffle, and truffle oil. Keep the leftovers to make arancini (see recipe on next page).

'ARANCINI WITH RAGÙ & MOZZARELLA'

about 1¼ cups leftover risotto
  (recipes on pages 92 and 93)
½ cup meat sauce (recipes on
  pages 80 and 82)
4 oz. mozzarella, cut into 10
  pieces
scant 1 cup all-purpose flour
1 egg, beaten
1 cup fine, dry bread crumbs
about 2 cups vegetable oil

I am a great believer in using up everything. Arancini must have been invented by a very clever Italian cook, because they use leftover meat sauce, any old cheese, and leftover risotto. They are great served with a green salad and spicy tomato sauce.

Take a generous tablespoonful of cold risotto and press it into the palm of your cupped hand. Put a teaspoon of meat sauce and a piece of mozzarella in the center and curl up your hand until you can shape the rice into a ball with the sauce and cheese sealed in the middle. Cover with some more risotto, rolling it all into a large ball. Repeat with the remaining risotto, sauce, and cheese, then refrigerate the balls to set.

Dust the risotto balls in flour, then dip them in the beaten egg and coat with the bread crumbs. Heat the oil in a deep fryer or wok. When the oil starts to shimmer, deep-fry the arancini, five at a time. If you are worried that they will not be hot all the way through, you can finish cooking them in a 350°F oven for about 10 minutes.

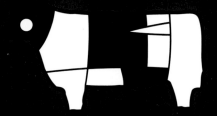

PIES STEWS & BRAISES

My father always said, "You can't beat a good pie, son!" No truer words have been spoken. Great pies are full of great filling, and the great fillings come from rich, slow-cooked beef. The cuts of beef that need this long, gentle cooking process are the tastiest ones by far. All you need is a Dutch oven, or other heavy pot with a lid, and the cooking will be carefree—you can walk away from the stove while the braise does its bit. The waiting game is rewarded when you lift that lid after hours of cooking and experience the first waft of delicious aromas. Don't be tempted to stir a good stew: all you will do is break it up, turning it to mush. But if you do, I suppose you could always make it into a pie!

'POTATO-TOPPED BEEF PIE'

refrigerated or homemade
  piecrust
1 egg, beaten
3 large potatoes, peeled and
  thinly sliced
3½ Tbs. butter, melted, for
  brushing

filling

3½ Tbs. butter
2 small onions, minced
2 lb. boneless beef chuck,
  without too much fat, chopped
1 cup beef stock (recipe on
  page 22)
½ cup all-purpose flour
2 thyme sprigs
2 Tbs. Worcestershire sauce
handful of chopped fresh
  parsley
salt and pepper
pinch of grated nutmeg

First make the filling. Melt the butter in saucepan. Add the onions and fry over medium heat until they soften. Add the beef and fry, pressing down with a fork, until it has browned. Drain off the pan juices, adding them to the stock.

Sprinkle the flour over the meat, stir, and continue cooking for 2 minutes. Remove the pan from the heat and gradually add the stock, mixing well. Return the pan to the heat and stir constantly until the mixture boils and thickens.

Add the thyme, Worcestershire sauce, parsley, salt, pepper, and nutmeg. Cover the pan and simmer over low heat for 30 minutes.

Heat the oven to 425°F. Line your pie pan with the piecrust and prick the bottom several times with a fork. Cover with a sheet of parchment paper and weigh down with dried beans. Bake for 20 minutes, then lift out the paper and beans and brush the pastry shell with beaten egg.

Turn the oven down to 375°F. Spoon the filling into the pastry shell and cover with the sliced potatoes. Brush the potato with lots of melted butter, then put the pie into the oven and bake for 50 minutes to 1 hour. Serve with ketchup.

'COTTAGE PIE'

1 Tbs. vegetable oil

2 medium onions, minced

3 large carrots, minced

4 celery ribs, minced

2 leeks, minced

2 garlic cloves, crushed

salt and pepper (black and white)

2 lb. ground beef (not too fine or fatty)

½ bunch of fresh thyme

½ bunch of fresh rosemary

2 bay leaves

⅔ cup all-purpose flour

2 cups beef stock

1 cup red wine

Worcestershire sauce

steak sauce

hot mashed potatoes (recipe on pages 218–219)

¼–½ cup (½–1 stick) butter

1 cup heavy cream

2 egg yolks

Whoever created this dish was a genius: ground beef, thick gravy, and vegetables, topped with soft mash under a crisp top. The filling needs to be well cooked and the layer of potato should be thick so that it does three jobs: taking up the sauce from underneath; staying soft, hot, and unctuous in the middle; and becoming crisp on top.

Put the oil in a large, heavy pan and start to cook the vegetables and garlic. When they smell like they are frying, add some salt and pepper, and cook for a few more minutes. Add the beef and fry over high heat for at least 10 minutes so it has some color. Tie the herbs together with string and drop into the pan. Sprinkle the flour over and cook, stirring well, for 5 minutes longer.

Slowly pour in the stock and red wine, then simmer until the sauce has reduced and become thick, about 1 hour. Take the pan from the heat and add Worcestershire and steak sauces to taste. Adjust the seasoning with salt and pepper. Pour the filling into a baking dish—it should only be half full.

Heat the oven to 375°F. When you make your mashed potatoes, please use white pepper to season. While the mash is hot, beat in some of the butter and the cream, then add the eggs—if beaten in well the eggs will make the mash rise as it cooks so that it is light with a crisp top.

Spoon the mash over the beef mix, filling the dish. Drop some small bits of butter on top and bake for 25 minutes—the edges will bubble a bit and the sauce come up the sides, which is fine.

'CORNISH PASTIES'

1 lb. potatoes, peeled and chopped

8 oz. turnips, peeled and chopped

3/4 cup chopped onions

salt and pepper

1 lb. boneless beef chuck, finely chopped

2 lb. puff pastry sheets (about 2 packages)

There are pasties and then there are true "paaarrstys," as they say in Cornwall, England. To make a great "paaarrsty," the vegetables need to be cut into pieces about the size of a postage stamp but a bit thicker— they don't have to be that even. This recipe makes about eight or ten pasties, and you can freeze them raw or cooked. Rest assured, however, that once cooked they will be eaten.

Mix together all the vegetables and season with lots of pepper and a little salt. Put them in a colander so the excess water can drain off while you do the rest.

Season the beef with lots of pepper and a little salt. Break up the meat a little so it is free-flowing rather than one big lump.

Heat the oven to 375°F. Cut the pastry sheets into 8-inch rounds. Spoon the vegetable mix into the center of the rounds, then sprinkle the meat over (yes, raw). The meat must be on top of the vegetables, or it will make the base of the pasties too soggy.

Dip your finger in some water and rub it around the edge of the pastry rounds, then fold them in half like a turnover, with the edges meeting at the top. Press to seal the edges together. Gently push the pastry ridge down, then either fold it over, or crimp or flute. Put the pasties on a baking sheet and bake for 45 minutes.

'AUNTY MARY'S SLOW-COOKED POTPIE'

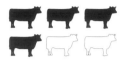

4 lb. beef for stew, such as skirt
   steak, boneless shank, brisket,
   or cheek, trimmed of excess fat
   (leave in all the gristle) and cut
   into 1¼-inch cubes
½ cup all-purpose flour
salt and pepper
¼ cup vegetable oil
2 large onions, roughly chopped
4 cups beef stock (recipe on
   page 22) or water
3½ Tbs. Worcestershire sauce
4 large potatoes, peeled and cut
   into 1¼-inch chunks

lard pastry
7 oz. lard, at room temperature
2⅔ cups self-rising flour, sifted
pinch of salt
¾ cup cold water
1 egg
a little milk

To make a great potpie, the meat has to be cooked long and slow. You want it to be moist and succulent, so only use beef that has plenty of sinew and a little fat. Then the pieces of meat will stay together and not be stringy. The pie filling is just as good on thick slices of hot buttered toast, so if your pie dish isn't big enough, keep the leftovers.

Shake the meat and flour in a plastic bag with some salt and pepper—a quick way to coat the meat in flour with no mess.

Heat a Dutch oven over medium heat and add the oil. When hot, fry the onions for about 3 minutes. Add the floured meat and cook until colored, about 10 minutes. Pour in the stock (or water) and add the Worcestershire sauce. Bring to a boil, then reduce the heat to a simmer and cook for about 2 hours.

Add the potatoes and cook gently for 1 hour longer.

Meanwhile, make the pastry: Rub the lard into the flour and salt, or mix in a food processor, until resembling bread crumbs. Add the water bit by bit and mix to a dough. Let rest for 20 minutes.

Check the meat—when ready it will be soft and break apart when squeezed. The sauce should be rich and thick. Season with salt and pepper as necessary.

Heat the oven to 375°F. Select a deep baking dish that has a rim. Fill the dish three-quarters with the meat mixture. Roll out the pastry to 1 inch thick and cut into a shape large enough to cover the top of the dish. Beat the egg and milk together and brush over the rim. Lay the crust over the dish and press the edges down firmly onto the rim to seal. Brush the crust with the egg wash, then cut a small hole in the middle to allow steam to escape. Bake for 40 minutes. If the edges of the crust become too brown during baking, protect with some foil.

Tip The potatoes are added to bulk out the meat, thereby making the pie more cost-effective, but more importantly they help to thicken the sauce.

'PARTY PIES'

pastry shells

3 cups all-purpose flour

1 tsp. salt

½ cup beef drippings

filling

4 Tbs. (½ stick) butter, plus
   extra for greasing

salt and pepper

2 lb. onions, minced

2 lb. ground beef

⅔ cup all-purpose flour

pinch of grated nutmeg

2 tsp. soy sauce

2 cups beef stock (recipe on
   page 22)

pastry lids

1 lb. puff pastry sheets

1 egg, beaten

As an Aussie, I have been privileged to grow up with the meat pie. Not just the grand ground-beef pie that is the stalwart of every Australian football game, but the party pie—small enough to hold and just two bites' worth. On serving, the lid is lifted and ketchup poured in before the lid is replaced (this ritual is paramount to the enjoyment of the pie). You can use this recipe to make one or several larger pies instead of tiny ones.

Make the pastry for the shells the night before. Sift the flour and salt into a bowl. Put the drippings in a saucepan with 1¼ cups water and heat, stirring, until the drippings melt. Remove from the heat. Make a well in the center of the dry ingredients and pour in the liquid, stirring to make a dough. Wrap the pastry in plastic wrap and let it rest in the refrigerator overnight.

To make the filling, melt the butter in a large frying pan and season with lots of pepper and some salt. Add the minced onions and cook, stirring, until soft but not brown, about 5 minutes. Add the beef and cook, stirring, for 5 minutes. Sprinkle the flour over, stir, and keep cooking for a few minutes. Add the nutmeg, then the soy sauce and stock, and bring to a boil. Simmer, stirring occasionally, for 10 minutes. Set aside to cool.

When ready to put the pies together, heat the oven to 475°F and grease the pie pans or baking dishes.

Roll out the pastry for the shells and cut out disks slightly larger than your pie pans. Line the pans with the pastry, then fill with the cold meat filling. Cut out lids from the puff pastry. Dampen the rims of the pastry shells with water and press the lids on to seal. Brush the puff pastry lightly with beaten egg.

Place the pies in the oven. Reduce the temperature to 375°F and bake until puffed and browned, 20–25 minutes.

'PIE FLOATERS WITH PEA SOUP'

4–6 meat pies (recipe on
  page 105)
ketchup

soup
2 Tbs. butter
1 shallot, diced
salt and pepper
1 heaped cup whole dried peas,
  soaked
1 cup beef stock (recipe on
  page 22)
1 cup shelled fresh green peas
  (or thawed frozen peas)

For this, you take a good Aussie meat pie and serve it in a bowl of pea soup—yes, really. To make it work, it needs a healthy dose of "dead horse," as my father used to call it—ketchup to you and me. He had a great little poem (if you could call it that) that he'd recite when topping his pie: "Shake and shake and shake the bottle; none will come and then a lot'll!"

Make the pies following the recipe on the previous page, but cut the pastry larger to fit pie pans that are 5–6 inches in diameter. Bake them for about 25 minutes.

To make the soup, melt the butter in a saucepan, add the diced shallot, and season with salt and pepper. Cook until the shallot is translucent but without color, about 3 minutes. Add the dried peas and a generous amount of salt and black pepper. Cover with the stock, bring to a boil, and cook for 20 minutes.

Add the fresh peas, bring back to a boil, and cook for 5 minutes. Purée the soup in a blender or food processor. Taste and season again as necessary.

Divide the soup among serving bowls and top with the cooked meat pies. Serve with ketchup.

'BOEUF À LA FICELLE'

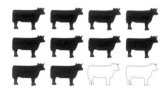

3-lb. boneless beef rump roast
4 leeks, white parts only
1 large onion, stuck with 1 clove
2 large carrots, peeled and
  chopped
2 large turnips, peeled and
  chopped
1 bouquet garni
salt and pepper

For this classic French dish, the beef has to be top quality and cut from the rump, which lies partially in the round and partially in the sirloin.

Tie a long piece of string around the beef roast, leaving the long ends hanging loose. Bundle the leeks together and tie them up, too. Put all the vegetables and the bouquet garni in a large pot with 3 quarts salted water. Bring to a simmer and cook for 1 hour.

Lower the meat into the pot, leaving the ends of the string hanging outside. Boil for 5 minutes, then reduce the heat and let simmer gently for 30 minutes.

Use the string to pull the meat from the pot. You will find it tender, rather underdone, and imbued with the flavor of the vegetables and herbs. If it is too rare for your taste, return it to the pot to cook for a few more minutes.

Discard the bouquet garni. Place the meat (whole or sliced) on a large, hot serving dish and surround with the vegetables. Spoon some of the cooking liquid over to moisten. Serve with potatoes and green beans.

'BEEF STROGANOFF'

1 lb. beef tenderloin
4 Tbs. vegetable or corn oil
salt and black pepper
12 button mushrooms, sliced
¼ cup brandy
½ cup heavy cream

spaetzle
⅔ cup all-purpose flour
1 egg
1 Tbs. warm milk
salt
melted butter

Properly cooked, beef stroganoff is a beautiful dish and great with spaetzle or mashed potatoes, or even mashed potatoes and a fried egg.

To make the spaetzle, mix the flour, egg, milk, and a little salt together to make a dough. Push the dough through a spaetzle sieve, if you have one; otherwise, use a colander; or fit a pastry bag with a small tip, fill it with the dough, and squeeze it out into matchstick lengths, like little short worms.

Bring a big pot of water to a boil and drop in the spaetzle—they take about 2 minutes to cook. Drain well, then drop them into some melted butter; season with salt and pepper and keep warm.

To make the stroganoff, cut the beef into thin strips the size of your little finger and put them in a big bowl. Heat your biggest and heaviest frying pan. Add the oil to the beef, season it really well with lots of pepper and some salt, and mix together. Drop the beef into the hot pan and do not touch it for 1 minute—let it sizzle. Only once the beef starts to brown should you stir it. Cook for another minute. Keep the heat high. Stir in the mushrooms and cook for 1 minute longer. By now the meat should have color but not be dry.

Add the brandy—it should sizzle. Strike a match and burn off some of the booze, but not all of it as you need a punch. The alcohol will help make a great sauce by picking up all the flavorsome bits stuck on the bottom of the pan.

Shake the pan gently and add the cream. Shake again and bring to a boil— it should boil fast—then serve, with the spaetzle.

'BEEF STEW & DUMPLINGS'

4 lb. beef for stew, such as
   boneless shank or chuck,
   diced
$2/3$ cup all-purpose flour
salt and pepper
2 Tbs. beef drippings or lard
8 oz. onions, sliced
$1\frac{1}{2}$ lb. potatoes, quartered
4 cups beef stock (recipe on
   page 22)

dumplings
1 heaped cup ground or finely
   chopped beef suet
$4\frac{2}{3}$ cups self-rising flour
$1\frac{1}{4}$ cups warm water

This simple but very delicious stew is a leave-it-to-cook wonder. Everything gets put into the pot, which then goes into the oven for 3 hours. I like to brown the meat first, because I think it helps the taste.

Heat the oven to 375°F. Trim any excess fat from the diced meat. Take a large plastic bag, put the flour in it, and season well with salt and pepper. Drop the meat into the bag and shake it like mad to coat all the pieces in the seasoned flour.

Melt the drippings or lard in a Dutch oven. Add the meat and onions and fry until browned, stirring all the time. Add the potatoes and stir. Pour in the stock (or you could use water) and stir, scraping the bottom of the pan to take up the flour and all the flavorsome bits stuck on.

Cover with a lid (or foil). Put the stew in the oven, reduce the heat to 275°F, and let cook for 3 hours.

To make the dumplings, mix the suet, flour, and some salt in a big bowl. Stir in the warm water—this will make a heavy mixture. Roll into balls about the size of golf balls.

Take about $\frac{1}{2}$ cup of gravy from the stew and put it in a saucepan with 2 cups water. Bring to a boil. You will need to cook the dumplings in batches, so drop half of them into the pan and cook for 10 minutes, turning so they cook evenly and puff up.

Lift the dumplings out of the broth with a slotted spoon and keep warm while you cook the remainder. You can either serve them in a bowl separately from the stew, or gently stir them into the stew before serving, which I think is better.

'BRAISED BEEF WITH STAR ANISE'

6 star anise

handful of cassia bark or a
    cinammon stick

2 lemongrass stalks

vegetable oil

1 boneless beef shank

2 cups beef stock (recipe on
    page 22)

handful of sliced galangal or
    ginger

2 fresh red chiles, seeds
    removed and sliced

6 lime leaves, torn (optional)

2 Tbs. fish sauce

½ cup light soy sauce

1 cup rock sugar

This works really well both hot, as a stew with noodles, or cold, sliced and served in a salad.

Rinse the star anise and cassia bark or cinammon stick thoroughly in a strainer, then toast in a wok or dry frying pan until dark (but not too dark) and fragrant. Transfer them onto a piece of cheesecloth and tie into a bundle so they will be easy to remove from the pot during cooking. Cut the lemongrass into pieces about 2 inches long and leave them unpeeled.

Heat a little bit of oil in a large pot and brown the beef shank over high heat until it is dark in color. Once dark, remove the meat and clean the pot.

Pour the stock into the pot and add the spice bag, galangal, lemongrass, chiles, lime leaves, fish sauce, soy sauce, and sugar. Bring to a boil, then add the meat and let it simmer gently for 2½ hours. Alternatively, you can cook in a 350°F oven; add more liquid as needed and turn the meat regularly.

Take the meat from the pot. Strain the sauce and return the meat to it. If you are going to serve the meat with noodles, shred it. To serve cold, chill the meat, then slice it very thinly and toss with a little of the sauce and some shredded raw vegetables.

'BEEF RENDANG WITH LEMONGRASS & GINGER'

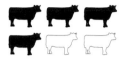

2 lemongrass stalks

$\frac{1}{3}$ cup coriander seeds

1 tsp. cumin seeds

1 tsp. ground turmeric

4-oz. block coconut cream

3 large onions, minced

6 garlic cloves, chopped

6 fresh red chiles, seeds removed and chopped

2 thumb-sized pieces fresh ginger, peeled and chopped

2 bay leaves

3 lb. beef for stew, cut into 1-inch cubes

2 cans (14 oz. each) coconut milk

2 cups strong veal or beef stock, heated

sticky (glutinous) rice for serving

This is a Muslim dish from Sumatra in Indonesia. By the time the big pot of liquid has cooked down to a kind of beef in jam, the meat is fabulously tender and melting. Shank is, for me, the very best cut to use here. The pot you use needs to be wide rather than deep, so that the liquid can evaporate as the beef cooks.

Pound the lemongrass to a pulp using a mortar and pestle. Gently toast the coriander and cumin seeds with the turmeric in a dry frying pan until fragrant, then grind to a powder (or pound with the mortar and pestle).

In a wide pan (I use a cast-iron wok), heat the block of coconut cream until it melts—keep the heat low so it does not burn. Drop in the onions, garlic, chiles, ginger, and pounded lemongrass. Cook gently until the onions have softened and the mixture starts to smell fragrant. Add the ground spices and bay leaves and fry for a few more minutes until the mixture is really aromatic.

Add the meat and increase the heat so it browns well all over, stirring to coat with the spices. Add the coconut milk and bring to a boil, then add the hot stock. Turn the heat up to high and continue cooking, stirring occasionally. The sauce will reduce to a thick paste and then will become thick like lava, really coating the meat—this will take at least an hour. Serve the rendang with sticky rice.

'BRAISED OXTAIL & CELERY-ROOT MASH'

2 oxtails, trimmed of excess fat
  and cut into chunks
salt and pepper
1/3 cup all-purpose flour
4 carrots
2 leeks
6 celery ribs
2 bunches of fresh flat-leaf
  parsley
2 small branches of fresh sage
about 6 Tbs. olive oil
14-oz. slab bacon, cut into large
  chunks
8 oz. veal shank, or 1 pig's foot
3 cups red wine

celery-root mash

1 large head celery root, peeled
  and diced
2 large potatoes, peeled and
  diced
1/2 cup milk
7 Tbs. olive oil
salt and pepper

Here long, slow cooking produces juicy, sticky meat that just has to be eaten with your fingers. My restaurant version of celery-root mash may seem a little over the top, but this root vegetable deserves special treatment. Beware of serving too much as it is very rich indeed. If you want to spice it up a little, add a chunk of fresh horseradish. The recipe also works with parsnips.

Heat the oven to 375°F. Season the oxtail well with salt and pepper and dust with flour. Tie the carrots, leeks, celery, and herbs tightly in a bundle.

Heat the olive oil in a Dutch oven. Add the bacon and cook for 2 minutes, then add the oxtail and let it sizzle. When well browned, turn the pieces over and cook for 3 minutes longer, making sure to move the bacon too so it doesn't burn.

When the meat is browned all over, add the bundle of vegetables and the shank or pig's foot. Add the wine and bring to a boil. Let it bubble away for about 10 minutes or so, while you scrape the sticky bits of meat from the bottom of the pot.

Pour in 2 quarts water, or enough almost to cover the meat. Carefully press a double sheet of parchment paper into the liquid to moisten it, then cover with the lid. Place in the oven and cook until the liquid has reduced right down and the meat is falling apart, about 3 1/2 hours.

To make the mash, put the vegetables in a heavy-based saucepan. Add the milk, olive oil, and seasoning with enough water to cover the vegetables. Bring to a boil and cook until the vegetables are all soft, 15–20 minutes. Drain off and reserve the cooking liquid. Mash the vegetables with a fork, then mix in enough of the reserved liquid to making the mash as sloppy as you like—the sloppier the better for me.

'DAUBE Á LA J.D.T.'

4 lb. boneless beef brisket

salt and pepper

olive oil

2 carrots, chopped

1 onion, chopped

1 celery rib, chopped

1 garlic clove, crushed

2 whole star anise

½ cup port

1¾ cups red wine

1 pig's foot

1¼ cups beef stock (recipe on
   page 22)

¼ cup dark soy sauce

1 cup Guinness®

2 Tbs. fish sauce

mashed potatoes (recipes on
   pages 218–219) for serving

To us, brisket is the classic cut for corned beef and pastrami. The French make braises from brisket on the bone, stewing it for long periods with pigs' feet to give a thick, gelatinous sauce. The recipe here is French in style, but the brisket is off the bone. Oxtail works well in this recipe, too, but takes a little longer to cook.

Heat the oven to 375°F. Trim most of the excess fat from the brisket, leaving some for color and flavor. Cut the meat into big hunks, about 2 inches square, and season really well with salt and pepper. Heat a little olive oil in a frying pan, add the brisket, and fry until well browned on all sides.

Heat some more oil in a Dutch oven. Add the vegetables, garlic, and star anise and cook briefly until the vegetables are just softened. Pour in the port and red wine, and let bubble until the liquid has reduced by half.

Add the brisket and pig's foot to the pot and cover with the stock. Bring to a boil. Skim any scum from the surface, then add the soy sauce, Guinness, and fish sauce. Transfer to the oven and cook until the meat is very tender, about 2 hours.

Take the pot from the oven, lift out the meat, and keep it warm. Strain the sauce and return to the pot along with the pig's foot. Bring to a boil and keep bubbling until the sauce is thick. Taste and adjust the seasoning as necessary.

Lift the pig's foot from the sauce and keep the meat from it to serve on toast (yum!). Drop the beef back into the sauce and return to the oven for a final 30 minutes of cooking. Serve with hot mashed potatoes.

'BOLLITO MISTO'

4 carrots
4 onions
4 celery ribs
1 pig's foot
3 branches of fresh sage
4 black peppercorns
2 lb. veal shank
2 lb. corned beef
1 chicken
sea salt
1 cotechino, or similar sausage
1 zampone
2 lb. cooked, pickled beef tongue

for serving
John's green sauce (recipe on
   page 120)
mostarda di frutta

For a modern bollito misto, boil gently but not too long, without stirring things around, so that all the meats and vegetables stay whole and you hit a balance of great stock and tender meat that retains all its flavor. The classic Italian way to serve bollito misto is with *salsa verde* (green sauce) and *mostarda di frutta* (fruits preserved in a mustard-flavored syrup). You can buy *mostarda di frutta* from any good Italian market. This is also where you will find the cotechino (a fresh pork sausage) and zampone (seasoned pork encased in a boned pig's foot).

Put the whole vegetables and pig's foot in the largest pot you can find. Cover with cold water, then add the sage and peppercorns. Bring to a boil, to "wash" the foot, then discard the water.

Add the veal shank and corned beef and cover with fresh water. Cook at a slow simmer for about 2 hours, skimming regularly.

Add the chicken and more cold water to cover. Bring to a boil again, then turn the heat back down. Simmer gently until all the meat is cooked, about 1½ hours, skimming as before. Taste the broth and add salt, if necessary.

Add the cotechino, zampone, and tongue, and pour in more cold water so everything is immersed. Bring to a boil, skimming well, then turn the heat down. Simmer until the sausages and tongue are heated through, about 30 minutes. The broth should be rich and clear.

Remove the meats, place on platters, and cut into chunky pieces. Take out the vegetables, cut them into small pieces, and put into a serving dish. Put the meats and vegetables on the table with bowls of green sauce and *mostarda di frutta*, and let everyone help themselves to the feast.

'JOHN'S GREEN SAUCE'

Makes about 3 cups

½ bunch of fresh flat-leaf
  parsley, stems removed
2 bunches of fresh basil, stems
  removed
bunch of fresh mint, stems
  removed
bunch of fresh tarragon, stems
  removed
2 slices stale bread
½ cup red-wine vinegar
2 large shallots
2–3 garlic cloves
⅓ cup capers, drained
3 canned anchovy fillets,
  drained
1 heaped Tbs. Dijon mustard
1 hard-cooked egg, shelled
2 cups olive oil
salt and pepper

Blend the parsley, basil, mint, and tarragon in a food processor. Remove and place in a large bowl.

Soak the bread in the vinegar. Mince the shallots and garlic and add them to the herbs. Roughly chop the capers and anchovies and add to the herbs.

Blend the soaked bread and mustard together in the food processor, then add them to the herb mixture. Finely grate the egg and add to the mix, then pour in the olive oil and season to taste with salt and pepper.

The sauce will keep, covered with plastic wrap, in the refrigerator for 3–4 days. It is also good with roast chicken, soups, and toast.

'BRAISED BEEF CHEEK, CARROT PURÉE & SPRING VEGETABLES'

2 beef cheeks, about 1 lb. each
all-purpose flour for dusting
1 Tbs. vegetable oil
1 leek, halved
2 celery ribs
2 medium carrots
about 4 cups chicken stock
½ cup soy sauce
1 cup sake
flaked sea salt and white pepper
4–6 asparagus spears, halved
6 snow peas
4 baby carrots
large handful of spinach leaves
12 canned butter or lima beans,
    halved and heated

Clean the beef cheeks, then remove the silvery skin by running a knife underneath it—a bit like skinning a fish. Cut each one into four pieces and dust lightly with some flour. Heat the oil in a frying pan, add the meat, and fry until browned.

Transfer the browned meat to a large pot. Add the leek, celery, and medium carrots and cover with the chicken stock. Add the soy sauce and sake. Bring to a rolling boil, then reduce the heat so that the liquid barely simmers and cook for about 1 hour.

Once the carrots are soft, remove them from the pot and purée in a food processor. Adjust the purée to your desired consistency with more stock, then add salt and white pepper to taste.

Keep cooking the beef cheeks over low heat until tender, taking care not to overcook—the meat is done if it falls apart readily when tested with a fork. Remove the beef cheeks to a plate and cover with another plate to weight them down.

Return the pot to the heat, bring the liquid to a boil, and reduce to the consistency of a gravy. Meanwhile, in a saucepan of boiling salted water, blanch the asparagus, snow peas, baby carrots, and spinach separately—about 1–2 minutes for the firm vegetables and just a few seconds for the spinach leaves. Drain well.

To serve, place a little spinach on each serving plate. Top with the beef cheeks and spoon some carrot purée on the beef. Arrange the asparagus, snow peas, baby carrots, and butter beans on the carrot purée and spoon some sauce over all.

'STEAK & KIDNEY PUDDING'

4 lb. boneless beef shank

salt and pepper

2 carrots

1 leek

3 celery ribs

bunch of fresh flat-leaf parsley

1 small branch of fresh sage

3 Tbs. olive oil

about 7-oz. slab bacon, cut in chunks

1 veal shank or pig's foot

about 1½ cups red wine

4 lamb kidneys

suet dough

2⅓ cups all-purpose flour

½ cup (1 stick) butter, plus extra for greasing

½ cup ground or finely chopped beef suet

1 tsp. salt

½ tsp. sugar

1–2 Tbs. warm water

You can use beef or lamb kidneys for this traditional British recipe. For the meat, I've used beef shank with some veal shank or pig's foot, which makes the sauce thick and unctuous. You can discard the pig's foot after cooking; or, take the bone out, roll the meat up in plastic wrap, and refrigerate to firm it up, then slice and fry it for supper.

Heat the oven to 375°F. Cut the beef into chunks about the size of your hand and season it generously—remember this is the base of the sauce and the filling so it needs to be seasoned really well. Tie the carrots, leek, celery, and herbs tightly in a bundle.

Heat the oil in a Dutch oven. Add the bacon and beef and let them sit and sizzle. Don't shake the pan or try to flip the beef too early, although you can move the bacon around. Wait until the beef is well browned underneath—the pieces can be lifted off when ready. Once you've browned both sides, add the vegetable bundle and the veal shank or pig's foot. Pour in the wine and bring to a boil, then let it reduce for about 10 minutes, scraping the sticky bits from the bottom of the pot.

Pour in about 2 quarts water, so that it almost covers the meat. Add the kidneys and stir well. Cover with parchment paper and carefully press this into the liquid to moisten it so that it doesn't burn. Transfer the pot to the oven. Cook until the liquid has reduced down and the meat is virtually falling apart, about 2½ hours. Change the parchment paper once during cooking, because it will have absorbed all the fat and impurities, to leave a lovely clear, shiny sauce.

Remove from the oven and let cool a little. Take out the kidneys, chop into thumb-sized pieces, and set aside in a bowl. Take out the vegetables, chop roughly, and mix with the kidneys. Take out the meat and chop, keeping it chunky. Remove the shank or foot.

Place the pot on the stovetop, bring the sauce to a boil, and reduce to a gravy consistency. Taste and season. Let cool.

To make the suet dough, combine all the ingredients in a bowl. Knead lightly to a smooth dough; try not to overwork it or the heat of your hands will melt the suet and the crust will be heavy. Roll out about one-third of the dough into a disk large enough to cover the top of a 2-quart ceramic pudding basin, steamed-pudding mold, or similar heatproof bowl; set aside. Grease the inside of the mold with a little butter. Cut a disk of parchment paper to fit the bottom of the mold, moisten it with water to make it pliable, and press inside. Roll out the remaining dough into a circle big enough to line the mold, leaving a little hanging over the rim. Press it gently into the mold. Add the kidney and vegetable mixture to the mold, then the meat, and then fill to the top with gravy (keep the remaining gravy to serve with the pudding). Put the pastry lid on top. Bring the overhanging pastry up over the top, moisten the underside with water, and press gently to seal. Cover the top with a double sheet of moistened parchment paper, tie with string, and wrap the whole thing in foil.

Put a folded dishtowel in the bottom of a large pot. Set the mold in the pan on the towel and add enough boiling water to come three-quarters of the way up the side of the mold. Put the lid on the pot and let simmer for about $4\frac{1}{2}$ hours, replenishing the water when necessary.

When the pudding is cooked, unwrap it and transfer it onto a serving plate. Pour some hot gravy over and serve.

STEAKS & BIG HUNKS

The mighty bovine is a versatile beast, providing cuts of all kinds. Laying along his back is the most prized hunk of meat of all—comprising the rib, short loin, and sirloin. Sitting inside the short loin is the tenderloin. Collectively this area is the least used or worked part of the beast, so the meat is tender, with fat that lays in the muscle and melts as it cooks—that's why it can be cut into steaks that cook quickly, or left in big hunks for roasting. It may seem just too traditional, but let me tell you: Done well, there are few things better than roast beef. A hunk of rib roasted in a hot oven will deliver flavor, texture, and aroma, and feed a whole family. In this chapter you will also learn to cook steak perfectly, but do me a favor: Relax and enjoy cooking it! If you feel you are not in control, your steak will misbehave. You are the master.

'HOW TO COOK A GREAT STEAK'

Cooking steak is a joy, because it is a terrific piece of meat with great flavor, whether grilled or fried. There are no rules, apart from this: Eat the steak cooked the way you like it and tell steak snobs to back off.

I suggest frying the more delicate steaks such as filet mignon and grilling the bigger, tastier, fattier ones like the rib-eye or anything on a bone, such as porterhouse or T-bone.

It is hard to say how long to cook a steak, because each one varies in thickness and structure. But generally, for medium steak, I'd sear for 2 minutes on each side, then cook a minute extra for each ⅜ inch or so of thickness. So a ¾-inch-thick sirloin served medium will take about 6 minutes in total. If there is a bone, it will be more like 2 minutes extra per ⅜ inch.

Frying

Use a solid pan that will hold the heat well, nothing flimsy. A black cast-iron skillet is perfect. Start by heating the skillet really well. If your steak is very thick (2–3 inches), heat the oven too, to 400°F, for finishing the cooking. Rub the steak with ample oil—vegetable oil is best. Season with salt and pepper after it is covered with oil or the salt will start to eat into the meat and dry it out.

Turn on the fan, because you are going to have lots of smoke. When the pan is so hot it is hard to put your hand close to it, drop in the steak. Don't touch it for 2 minutes. Then turn it over and, if it is not sizzling, add some more oil to the pan, but keep the heat high. Sear for 2 minutes longer, then turn again and finish the cooking.

If the steak is thick, put the pan in the oven. Cook for about 4 minutes, depending on the desired degree of doneness. You won't ever need to leave it in the oven for more than about 8 minutes; if you do it will be cremated.

Take the steak out and let it rest for 5 minutes—remember that the steak will continue to cook while it is resting. Drop a generous blob of butter in the pan before you set it aside. Pour the mix of melted butter and meat juices over the steak when you serve it.

Pan-grilling

Use a ridged cast-iron grill pan (also called a skillet grill or broiler pan). Set it over high heat 10 minutes before you even think about cooking. Meanwhile, rub the steak with oil and season it with salt and pepper on both sides.

Lay the steak on the grill pan and leave it for 2 minutes, then flip and sear the other side for 2 minutes. Continue cooking to the desired degree of doneness, then remove the steak and let it rest.

As with the fried steak, if it is really thick, finish the cooking in the oven, still in the grill pan.

Grilling over coals

To cook steaks over coals, follow the same principles as when using a grill pan, but keep an eye out for yellow flames. This means the fat has caught fire—you don't want the taste of burned fat on your meat, so move the steak to another part of the grill.

Creamed Horseradish

Just Mustard

Hollandaise Sauce

Broiled Mushrooms

Onion Rings

Béarnaise Sauce

Mustard Sauce

Cèpes Bordelaise Sauce

Creamed Horseradish

If you are able to find some fresh horseradish, use it for this sauce—a classic for beef. Buy a whole horseradish root; wrapped in plastic wrap, it will keep for a few weeks in the refrigerator. Alternatively, peel and grate the whole thing, then mix it with ½ cup white-wine vinegar and a pinch of salt. This can be stored in a tightly closed jar for weeks.

2 Tbs. grated horseradish in vinegar
½ cup sour cream
pinch of salt

Squeeze out any excess vinegar from the grated horseradish. Lightly whip the cream with the salt. Mix in the horseradish.

Just Mustard

If there ever was a marriage made in heaven, it has to be steak and mustard. Whoever it was that first made mustard was a very clever person indeed. There are a number of varieties available: English, which is the hottest; Dijon, which has a kick but is not as hot; American, which is mild; and plenty more. I'd go for English mustard with a full-bodied steak like a well-aged sirloin, and Dijon for a filet mignon. American mustard I reserve for hot dogs—beef hot dogs, that is, which are delicious!

Hollandaise Sauce

6 Tbs. white wine
6 Tbs. white-wine vinegar
20 black peppercorns
2 bay leaves
3 egg yolks
1¼ cups (2½ sticks) butter, melted and kept warm
pinch of salt
juice of ½ lemon

Boil the first 4 ingredients in a pan until reduced to about 3 tablespoons, 5–8 minutes. Let cool, then strain. Put the egg yolks in a large stainless steel bowl and set over a pan of barely simmering water. Whisk in a tablespoon of the vinegar reduction. Continue whisking until it turns pale and the whisk leaves a pattern in the sauce. Remove the bowl from the heat and gradually whisk in the butter. Add a tablespoon of water if you feel the sauce might be about to scramble. Beat in the salt and lemon juice. Serves 4.

Broiled Mushrooms

This is the best way I know to cook big, flat mushrooms. Remember, they are meaty in their own right, so should you have a friend who's (oh, am I going to say this...?) A VEGETARIAN (ahhhhhh!), you can always just serve them these mushrooms instead of a steak.

12 large portobello mushrooms
3–4 Tbs. olive oil
salt and pepper

Put the mushrooms on a rimmed baking sheet, stems facing up. Drizzle generously with olive oil. Sprinkle with salt and freshly ground black pepper. Broil slowly, at a good distance from the heat, until cooked. The mushrooms should be very dark in color but still very moist. Let cool a bit before serving.

Onion Rings

3 cups vegetable oil for deep-frying
½ cup soda water, chilled
1 cup cornstarch, plus extra for dusting
large pinch of salt
2 ice cubes
1 large white or brown onion, peeled and second
  layer removed

Heat the oil gently in a deep-fat fryer over medium heat. The oil will start to shimmer when ready. Whisk the soda water, cornstarch, and salt to a paste. Add the ice cubes and keep the batter cool.

Cut the onion into slices about ½ inch thick, separate into rings, and place in a large bowl. Pour boiling water over the rings and stir well. Drain and pat dry. Dust all the rings with extra cornstarch, then dip in the batter.

Drop the onion rings into the oil one at a time (fry about 10 per batch). When the onion rings float to the surface, keep cooking for another minute, then drain on paper towels. Serves 4.

Béarnaise Sauce

½ cup white-wine vinegar
1 shallot, chopped
a few sprigs of fresh tarragon
2 egg yolks
½ cup (1 stick) butter, melted and kept warm
salt and pepper

Put the vinegar, shallot, and tarragon in a saucepan and boil until the mixture has reduced by about three-quarters. Let cool, then pour into in a large stainless steel bowl.

Set the bowl over a pan of barely simmering water. Add the egg yolks and whisk until you can see the whisk leaving a pattern in the sauce.

Remove the bowl from the heat and start to add the melted butter, little by little, whisking all the time, until all the butter is used, or your arm has fallen off! Sitting the bowl on a folded dishtowel will help to keep the heat in. Season with salt and plenty of pepper. Serves 2.

Mustard Sauce

This has to be one of the simplest but best mustard sauce recipes ever. I have used it for everything from beef to veal to kidneys and even roast squab. This recipe makes enough for four steaks with some left over to be served cold on things like cold roast beef.

1½ cups heavy cream
1½ cups Dijon mustard
handful of chopped fresh parsley

Put the cream in a heavy-based saucepan, bring it to a boil, and let it boil for a few minutes, until reduced by about half. Whisk in the mustard. Take the pan from the heat, throw in the parsley, and give it a stir to mix.

Cèpes Bordelaise Sauce

2 Tbs. vegetable oil
4 Tbs. (½ stick) butter
2 large shallots, minced
1 garlic clove, crushed to paste
14 oz. fresh cèpes (porcini mushrooms)
1 cup good red wine
1 thumb-sized piece bone marrow (optional)
2 handfuls of chopped fresh parsley

Heat a large pan and add the oil and the butter. Cook the shallots gently for a few minutes, stirring, until soft—don't let them brown. Add the garlic and continue to cook, stirring often. Slice the cèpes the width of your little finger. Drop them into the pan. Stir, shake, and cook for 5 minutes. Add the wine and the bone marrow (if using). Boil for 3 minutes, then take the pan off the heat and add the parsley.

For a richer sauce you can finish with a few drops of cream.

'CÔTE DE BOEUF WITH CARAMELIZED SHALLOTS'

2 *côte de boeuf* or big cowboy
    steaks (see page 18), weighing
    about 1½ lb. each
pepper

caramelized shallots
¼ cup vegetable oil
12 large shallots
3½ Tbs. butter
2 bay leaves
1 fresh thyme sprig
flaked sea salt
1 cup beef or veal stock
    (see recipes on page 22 or 24)

Each of these bone-in rib-eye steaks is big enough to serve two. I often cook them with all the fat so I get maximum flavor, then trim off some of the fat before carving. I don't think the steak should be too rare— medium is what I prefer.

Heat the oil in a frying pan, add the whole shallots, and color them over high heat. Once colored, drain off and throw away the oil. Add the butter, bay leaves, thyme, and some salt to the pan. Cook for about 5 minutes, turning and shaking the shallots; try not to burn the butter.

Add enough stock just to cover the bottom of the pan and let the liquid bubble away before adding any more; the sauce will reduce and become sticky while cooking the shallots at the same time. Continue until the shallots are very soft and have a thick buttery and beefy glaze.

Meanwhile, heat a ridged cast-iron grill pan or broiler pan until very hot (about 10 minutes). Preheat the oven to 400°F. Season the steaks well with pepper and score the fat a little. Place the steaks fat-side down in the grill pan. The fat will start to melt and this is what is going to flavor the outside of the meat.

Once the fat starts to char, let the steaks fall naturally onto one side. Cook for 4 minutes. Turn the steaks over and cook the other side for 4 minutes. Turn over again, but also rotate the steaks 180 degrees, then cook for 2 minutes longer. Flip the steaks over again, rotating as before. Place the pan in the oven to finish cooking for about 6 minutes for a medium steak. Let them rest for 5 minutes before serving them whole, with carving done at the table.

'BIG FRIES'

6 large potatoes
corn or vegetable oil for
  deep-frying
salt

Peel the potatoes and cut them into fries 1¼ inches thick. Soak them in cool water for 5 minutes, then change the water and soak for 5 more minutes. Place on a dishtowel and pat dry.

Meanwhile, put oil into a deep-fat fryer (depending on its size, you may have to cook in batches). The first stage is blanching the potatoes in oil, which is done in restaurants to produce fries that are well cooked and fluffy on the inside but crisp on the outside. To do this, heat the oil to 275°F. Place the potatoes in the oil and cook for 8–10 minutes. Lift them from the oil and drain well, then place them on a tray to cool.

The next stage of the cooking is the frying. This process should be quick and the oil must be hotter. The quantity of potatoes added to the oil will determine how quickly it is able to return to the temperature required to brown the outside of the fries and make the inside all fluffy.

Heat the oil to 375°F. Lower the potatoes into the oil and leave to fry for 2 minutes. Give them a little shake or stir, then continue frying until they are well colored and crisp, 4–5 minutes longer. Take the fries from the oil and drain thoroughly for a few minutes before putting them in a bowl and sprinkling with salt.

'STEAK SANDWICHES WITH ARUGULA & PARMESAN'

6 boneless sirloin steaks,
    about 5 oz. each
2 Tbs. vegetable oil
salt and pepper
4 oz. Parmesan cheese
1 small loaf of unsliced bread,
    multigrain or white and crusty
butter for spreading
4 oz. arugula (about 2 cups)

This has been a staple dish at Smiths since the day we opened. It is a perfect combination—juicy steak with peppery arugula and strong Parmesan. The bread will soak up the meat juices for you to enjoy. The sandwiches can be eaten as soon as they are made, or taken out for a picnic.

Using a rolling pin or meat mallet, bash the steaks so they are about 1 inch thick.

Heat a ridged cast-iron grill pan or broiler pan over high heat (or prepare the grill). Rub the steaks well with oil and place on the hot pan (or grill). Season with salt and pepper and sear for 2 minutes on the first side, then turn and cook to the desired degree of doneness—I cook mine for only 4 minutes in all, because I like a rare-ish steak.

Meanwhile, shave the Parmesan using a vegetable peeler, as if you were peeling a carrot.

Cut 12 slices from the bread and butter well. Lay six pieces out on the work surface, butter-side up. Scatter a little Parmesan over and put the cooked steaks on top. Cover with the remaining Parmesan, then pile on the arugula. Place the other pieces of bread on top. For the sandwiches to hold together, you need to press down on them firmly. Finally, cut them in half and wrap in wax paper—they will keep for a few hours that way.

'PEPPER STEAK'

⅓ cup black peppercorns

4 filet mignon steaks, about
8 oz. each

5 Tbs. butter

3 Tbs. beef stock (recipe on
page 22)

4 Tbs. brandy

1 Tbs. heavy cream (optional)

This is one steak dish that is best with filet mignon, because you need that thickness to give the right ratio of meat to pepper—otherwise it will be uncomfortably hot. I like this steak served with just the buttery, peppery juices, but some people like to add a touch of cream at the end. It's up to you.

Crush the peppercorns in a food processor or with a mortar and pestle, then sieve them to remove all the dust, which will otherwise catch in your throat. Press the crushed peppercorns into both sides of the steaks.

Heat 3 tablespoons of the butter in a heavy skillet over medium heat. Add the steaks and leave them alone until you can see they are forming a golden crust underneath. Turn them over and cook until medium-rare—about 3 minutes on each side, or longer if you prefer them medium.

Remove the steaks from the pan and keep them warm. Raise the heat under the pan, add the stock and the brandy, and flame it carefully to burn off the alcohol. Whisk in the rest of the butter, scraping the bottom of the pan to incorporate all the tasty scraps. If using cream, add it to the sauce now. Either way, bring the sauce briefly to a boil, then pour it over the steaks to serve.

ALSO GOOD WITH STEAK: Big chunks of roast parsnip and carrot 🐄 Sticky 🐄 Ratatouille 🐄 New potatoes, rosemary, and lots of black pepper

'BREAKFAST STEAK WITH EGGS, MUSHROOMS & TOAST'

1 lb. large portobello mushrooms

7 Tbs. vegetable oil

salt and pepper

2 shallots, diced

2 garlic cloves, chopped

2 handfuls of fresh flat-leaf
parsley, chopped

4 eggs

4 boneless sirloin steaks, about
6 oz. each

4 thick slices sourdough bread

1 lemon, halved

Mushrooms on toast—very thick, well-buttered toast— is good for breakfast. Add a few eggs, some herbs, and seasoning, and it's even better. But if you add a good piece of steak, it becomes a feast that you can enjoy at any time of day. You need really large mushrooms for this, as big as saucers.

Heat the broiler. Place the mushrooms stem-side up on a baking sheet, drizzle with 3 tablespoons of the oil, and season with salt and pepper. Broil for 8–10 minutes. Remove and let cool slightly.

Set a ridged cast-iron grill pan or broiler pan over high heat and let it heat up for 10 minutes. Meanwhile, put 3 tablespoons of oil in a large frying pan. Add the shallots and cook for 2 minutes, then add the garlic and cook for 2 more minutes. Remove from the pan and set aside.

Slice the mushrooms thickly. Add them to the frying pan and let them cook, without moving, until browned underneath, about 4 minutes. Turn and cook for 2 minutes longer. Season and add the cooked shallots and garlic, along with the parsley.

Rub the steaks with oil and season well on both sides. Place in the grill pan and sear for 2 minutes, then flip and sear for 2 minutes on the other side. Continue cooking to the desired degree of doneness, then set the steaks aside to rest.

Arrange the mushrooms into four circles, each with a hole in the center. Crack an egg into each hole (add more oil if the pan is getting too dry). Cook until the white is firm but the yolk still soft.

Toast the bread. Squeeze some lemon juice on the steaks to serve.

fried onions and fried egg 🐄 Eggplant and black bean sauce
🐄 Tomato, mozzarella, and basil salad 🐄 Creamy mash and mustard

'CARPET BAG STEAK'

4 filet mignon steaks, about
   6 oz. each
8 fresh oysters in the shell
4 large slices bacon
vegetable oil
salt and pepper
¾ cup (1½ sticks) butter, cut
   in pieces

This is an Australian classic—tender steak stuffed with fresh oysters, then wrapped in strips of bacon. It is important to retain all the oyster juices, because they will keep the oysters lovely and moist, and the saltiness will flavor the meat.

Take each steak and insert a sharp knife into the side to make a pocket—not cutting all the way through.

Shuck the oysters and release them from their shells, draining off and keeping the juices. Put four oysters back in their half shells to serve alongside the steaks. Take the other oysters and put one inside the pocket of each steak. Pour in some of the juices.

Wrap a slice of bacon around each steak and stick a wooden toothpick in to hold it all together. Put a heavy skillet on the heat and get it super-hot. Rub the steaks all over with oil and season with salt and a little pepper.

Put the steaks in the pan and sear for about 3 minutes each side, then turn the heat down and cook for 2 more minutes on each side. (If you want the steaks to be well done, the cooking will need to be finished in a 400°F oven for about 5 minutes.) Add the butter and the remaining oyster juices to the pan and bubble up while scraping up all the tasty bits from the bottom.

Serve your steaks with fries (page 134) and a tomato salad.

'SURF 'N' TURF'

6 filet mignon steaks, about
   8 oz. each
olive oil
salt and pepper
20 raw langoustines, shelled
2 garlic cloves, chopped
6 Tbs. butter
juice of 1 lemon, plus 1 lemon,
   quartered, for serving
1 Tbs. fresh tarragon leaves

The seafood for this classic is usually lobster, but I've used langoustines (also marketed as scampi, Dublin Bay prawns, or lobsterettes). You can substitute lobster if you prefer, or even big shrimp. The tarragon and lemon make a big difference to the flavor.

Heat the oven to 350°F and place a heavy skillet over high heat. Rub the steaks with olive oil, then add to the pan and season well with salt and pepper. Sear on both sides for 5 minutes, then transfer the pan to the oven to cook for about 6 minutes. The result will be rare. Set aside to rest for 5 minutes while making the sauce.

Put the skillet back on the stovetop, adding 2 teaspoons olive oil. Drop the langoustines into the pan and cook for 2 minutes, then turn and cook for 2 more minutes. Remove the langoustines from the pan and place in a warmed serving dish.

Add the garlic and half the butter to the pan and let melt over medium heat for 1 minute. Add the remaining butter and cook until it starts to brown, about 2 minutes longer. Pour in the lemon juice and stir in the tarragon, then pour the sauce over the langoustines.

Place the steaks on serving plates and spoon the sauce and the langoustines over the top. Serve with salad and lemon wedges.

'GRATIN DAUPHINOISE'

3 lb. russet or baking potatoes

5 cups milk

freshly grated nutmeg

sea salt and ground white
    pepper

2 Tbs. unsalted butter

1 cup heavy cream

1 cup grated Gruyère cheese

1 garlic clove, halved

Heat the oven to 375°F. Thinly slice the potatoes and put them in a large saucepan with the milk, some nutmeg and salt, and half the butter. Bring to a boil, stirring occasionally, and cook until the potatoes are tender, about 10 minutes.

Mix together most of the cream and half the grated cheese. Add this mixture to the potatoes.

Rub the bottom of a baking dish with the remaining butter and the garlic. Pour the potatoes in their creamy mixture into the dish. Scatter the remaining cheese over the top, then pour on the last of the cream. Bake until tender, bubbling, and golden brown, 1–1¼ hours.

Let the dauphinoise settle for 10 minutes before serving in the dish. Or you can serve it as we do in the restaurant: When the dauphinoise has cooled down, hold an upturned rimmed baking sheet on top of the dish and turn it over so the dauphinoise is unmolded onto the sheet. Cut the dauphinoise into squares (we set them on parchment paper so it is easy to reheat them individually). When ready to serve, reheat in a 425°F oven until hot through, 5–10 minutes.

'T-BONE STEAK WITH TURNIP & MUSTARD GRATIN'

4 T-bone steaks, about 1 lb. each
vegetable oil
salt and black pepper

turnip gratin
butter for greasing
1 lb. turnips
1 cup heavy cream
¼ cup crème fraîche
¼ cup Dijon mustard
1 cup grated Gruyère cheese

Both the T-bone and porterhouse are extraordinary steaks, because they include both the tenderloin and the strip loin. We cut them quite thin and like that they take 8–12 minutes to cook in a grill pan. The Italians love them really thick and grilled over charcoal. Those steaks are far too big for one person (unless he is a huge eater).

Heat the oven to 425°F and butter a baking dish that is 2–3 inches deep. Peel and slice the turnips, then let them soak in a bowl of cold water while you continue with the rest of the preparation.

Bring the cream to a boil in a saucepan and immediately take the pan off the heat. Stir in the crème fraîche and mustard.

Drain the turnips and return to the bowl. Cover with boiling water and let blanch for 2 minutes. Drain well. Gently mix the cream mixture with the turnips, then pour into the buttered dish. Sprinkle with the cheese. Tap the dish so it all settles down, then bake until tender and really brown on top, about 20 minutes.

While the gratin is in the oven, cook the steaks. Heat a ridged cast-iron grill pan over high heat for 10 minutes. Rub the steaks with oil and season both sides with salt and pepper, then place in the grill pan. Sear for 2 minutes, then flip and sear the other side for 2 minutes. Continue cooking to the desired degree of doneness (you can put really thick steaks in the oven, in the grill pan, to finish cooking), then let rest for a few minutes.

Serve with the turnip gratin. T-bones also taste great with gratin dauphinoise (page 142).

'

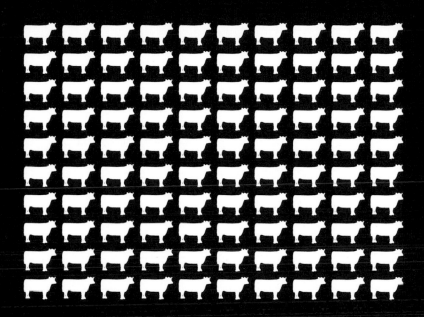

'

The ritual of cooking meat on a spit is a man's thing and it should probably stay that way! It involves getting the biggest piece of meat that you can find—maybe even a whole beast if it is a pig or lamb—and cooking it long and slow, impaled on a metal spit, turning constantly over a fire of some sort. The best spit-roasters have a cover and the cover is important—the meat needs to be enclosed so it can cook gently but in a good amount of heat.

My choice for spit-roasting is what I call a butt of beef, which is the whole round (the entire upper leg) plus the hindshank, all on its massive bone. The night before cooking, make up a rub for the outside of the meat. It will never penetrate, but that's okay. The crisp, salty, herby exterior is reserved for the master carver and his friends. We call it carver's rights! Mix together two generous handfuls of salt, a handful of ground black pepper, a generous handful of chopped fresh rosemary, 10 crushed garlic cloves, and 1 cup oil. Rub the mixture all over the beef.

Next day you have to impale it. This is a serious business because, as the meat cooks, it will give way. If not secured properly, the rod in the middle will be turning but the meat will not. Once that spit starts turning, you should not stop it, or the meat will be well done on one side and raw on the other.

If you are lucky, you may be able to find a butcher who will put the meat on the spit for you. Otherwise, just avoid the bone, trying to insure that the spit comes out as far toward the hoof end as possible. I find a couple of big lengths of garden wire really useful for trussing the beef up if it starts to come away.

After about 6 hours of roasting you will have 4 inches or so of properly cooked meat. Although the bone acts as a conductor of heat, you will nevertheless need to eat the beef in shifts—but that is part of the fun.

Okay, now to carving. The best way is to keep the heat on low, and to stop and start the spit as you carve. Very few gatherings will be able to devour the whole butt and very few people can cook the whole thing all the way through to the bone without the exterior drying out, so expect to leave it to cook for 1 hour or so longer once you get close to the bone.

Simply select a place and start carving the beef from right to left, keeping the knife flat and making the slices thin. As you carve, stack the meat on metal trays and keep it hot at the bottom of the spit—unless your guests are already helping themselves.

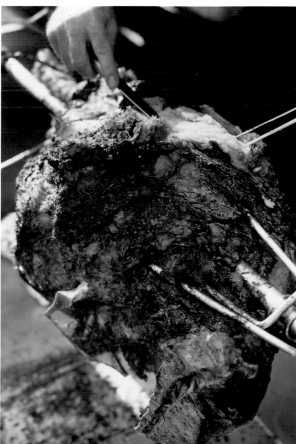

'BEST BREAKFAST BAPS'

1 lb. potatoes, peeled and
quartered

about 6 cups bread flour, plus
extra for dusting

4 tsp. salt

½ cup lard, cubed

2 packages quick-rising active
dry yeast

2 tsp. sugar

2 tsp. vegetable oil

If you want to serve these soft, homemade rolls at your party, it's better to make this recipe nine or ten times rather than try to tackle one gigantic batch. The recipe is easily halved, too, but I always make it all, because I like the baps toasted the next day with butter, Vegemite, and sharp Cheddar. The baps can be made a few days in advance and then gently warmed if need be; they can also be frozen.

Cook the potatoes in a pan of boiling water until tender. Drain, reserving 1 cup of the cooking liquid, and set aside to cool. Put 5½ cups of the flour and the salt in a mixing bowl and rub in the lard. Add the yeast and sugar to the cooled cooking liquid and stir well. Mash the potatoes.

Mix the potatoes into the flour, then add the yeast liquid and mix in enough of the remaining flour to form a soft dough. Turn onto a floured surface and knead until smooth and elastic, about 10 minutes. Alternatively, knead the dough in a machine on medium speed for 4 minutes.

Lightly oil a large bowl. Place the dough in the bowl, turning it so that the ball is oiled all over. Cover the bowl with a damp cloth and let rise somewhere warm until doubled in volume, about 1½ hours.

Lightly flour two heavy baking sheets. Punch down the dough and turn it onto a floured surface. Divide into 12 pieces and roll each into a ball. Place the balls on the baking sheets, keeping them evenly spaced. Cover with a dishtowel and let rise until puffy, about 40 minutes.

Heat the oven to 400°F. Use a rolling pin to gently flatten each ball into a 4-inch circle. Sprinkle with flour, then bake until the rolls are golden brown on top and sound hollow when tapped on the base, about 20 minutes.

'PORTERHOUSE WITH FRIED SALSIFY & BÉARNAISE SAUCE'

4 porterhouse steaks, about
  1 lb. each
vegetable oil

fried salsify

2 lb. salsify (oyster plant)
squeeze of lemon juice
1/3 cup all-purpose flour
1 egg
4 tsp. milk
3 handfuls of fresh bread
  crumbs
salt and pepper

for serving

bouquet of watercress
Béarnaise sauce (recipe on
  page 131)

I like porterhouse cooked rare, but—as I've already said—there's nothing wrong with having your steak any way you want, as long as it's not dry. If steak is overcooked and dry, you might as well eat a chunk of cardboard soaked in gravy.

Peel the salsify and keep it in a bowl of water with some lemon juice to prevent it from going brown. Bring a large saucepan of water to a boil. Cut the salsify into pieces 4 inches long and add them to the boiling water. Cook until tender, about 15 minutes, then drain and spread out on paper towels to drain and cool.

Lay out three wide but not too deep bowls—one with the flour, one with the egg and milk beaten together, and one with the bread crumbs. Dust the salsify in the flour, then dip it in the egg mixture, and finally roll in the bread crumbs until evenly coated. Keep refrigerated until you are ready to proceed.

Heat a heavy skillet until hot. Rub the steaks with oil, then sear for 2 minutes on each side. Continue cooking them to the desired degree of doneness, then remove from the pan and set aside to rest while you cook the salsify: Add 1/2 cup oil to the pan and fry the salsify until crisp and golden brown. Drain it briefly on paper towels, then serve with the steaks, watercress, and sauce.

'FILET MIGNON, BONE MARROW & PARMESAN'

4 slices white bread

2 Tbs. vegetable oil

4 filet mignon steaks, about
  8 oz. each

4 pieces of straight leg bone
  with marrow (optional)

sauce

2 cups good chicken stock

½ cup freshly grated Parmesan
  cheese

½ cup diced raw bone marrow

15 arugula leaves

salt and pepper

There are few dishes that I can call truly my own, but this is one I can claim. I devised it and then tested and played with it before we opened Mezzo in 1995, and it sat proud on the menu the whole time I was there.

Heat the oven to 350°F.

Cut a disk from each slice of bread to make a croûton about the same size as the steaks. Heat the oil in a heavy skillet and fry the croûtons until golden and crisp on both sides. Remove and drain on paper towels.

Pour the oil from the skillet and return it to high heat. When it is hot, add the steaks and season well with salt and pepper. Sear on both sides for 5 minutes, then transfer the pan to the oven to finish cooking for about 5 minutes. The result will be rare. If using the pieces of marrow bone, put them in a roasting pan and roast them alongside the steaks for 5 minutes.

Remove the steaks from the oven and let rest for 5 minutes while you make the sauce.

Bring the stock to a boil in a saucepan. Whisk in the Parmesan and then the diced bone marrow. Do not let the sauce return to a boil. Add the arugula, stirring until wilted. Season with salt and pepper to taste.

Place a croûton on each serving plate. Sit a steak on top and garnish with a piece of bone marrow scooped from the bone, if using. Pour the sauce over and serve.

'CLASSIC CHATEAUBRIAND'

handful of white peppercorns
2-lb. center-cut tenderloin roast
¼ cup vegetable oil
3 Tbs. butter
2 Tbs. Cognac
⅓ cup dry white wine
⅓ cup game or veal stock
⅔ cup heavy cream
salt

A chateaubriand always impresses! I like to coat it with peppercorns, but you don't have to use them—roast it plain if you prefer, and eat hot or cold.

Heat the oven to 450°F. Crush the peppercorns using a pestle and mortar, then press them into the meat to cover all sides.

Heat the oil and butter in a roasting pan and add the meat. Place in the oven and roast for 20 minutes, basting frequently. Remove from the oven and transfer the meat to a carving board or platter. Cover it with a sheet of buttered parchment paper to keep it hot.

Drain the cooking fat from the pan, then set the pan over high heat. Add the Cognac and let bubble, stirring, to deglaze, then add the white wine. Bring to a boil and let it reduce by half. Add the stock and return to a boil, then stir in the cream. Let the sauce reduce to a good consistency, stirring all the time.

Pour in the juices that have run out of the meat. Stir the sauce and taste for seasoning, adding salt if needed. Don't add pepper!

Carve the meat into 12 pieces. Coat with the hot sauce, including all the peppercorns that have fallen off during cooking.

'STEAK TARTARE'

1½ lb. tenderloin tail

large bunch of fresh parsley, chopped

4½ Tbs. Worcestershire sauce

⅓ cup ketchup

salt and pepper

½ heaped cup capers, finely chopped

1 cup minced shallots

4 egg yolks

Tabasco® sauce for serving

The great steak tartare can only be made with one cut of beef and that is the tenderloin. If anyone tells you anything different, they are WRONG!! Also, the meat should never be ground—it should be chopped by hand until it is finely minced. (You will find that using a large chopping knife is a great way to get rid of the frustrations of the day.) Let everyone mix their own tartare at the table, because we all like it different, don't we? I think this dish is best served with toast and salty fries. Oh, by the way, you can grill the patties, to make a good spicy hamburger.

Cut the meat into matchstick-thin strips, then bundle them up, turn them around 180 degrees, and cut into little cubes. Start chopping the meat and continue until it eventually forms into a ball on the board.

Mix the meat with some of the parsley, the Worcestershire sauce, a little of the ketchup, and some pepper. Spoon it onto serving plates and shape into a mound. The remaining ingredients should be arranged around the meat, and an egg yolk placed in the centre of each serving. This allows everyone to add and mix and season to their taste.

Tip Refrigerating the meat mixture, making sure it is very cold, will help the burgers bind together and stay moist during cooking.

'THE GREAT BURGER'

A great burger should be big and juicy, even when it is cooked well done. To make sure of this result, here are a couple of tricks:

1 A good burger needs fat, which is why I recommend using ground chuck rather than leaner round. You need fat to keep the meat moist while grilling.

2 My other secret is to use Chinese oyster sauce for seasoning instead of salt. I think salt makes the mixture dry and crumbly, because it draws the water from the meat.

Mix the beef, onions, and parsley together in a bowl. Add the oyster sauce and ketchup, then the egg yolk. Mix well, kneading until thoroughly combined. Divide the mixture into six equal portions and roll each one into a large ball. Refrigerate for at least 1 hour.

To cook, prepare the grill (by preheating on high for 10 minutes with the lid closed), or heat a ridged cast-iron grill pan or broiler pan over medium heat. Do not add oil.

Place the burgers on the grill or in the pan and leave for a few minutes until the edges start to color. Slide a metal spatula under each burger and turn it over. Brown the other side.

Turn the burgers again. If grilling, move them to the side or another area where it is slightly cooler; if using a grill pan, reduce the heat under it. Let the burgers cook for 15 minutes longer if you want them to be well done.

Serve your burgers with whatever you want. At Smiths we top our burgers with a piece of broiled bacon and a slice of Cheddar, and put them under the broiler for a few minutes until the cheese has melted, then serve in toasted buns spread with mayonnaise.

3 lb. ground chuck
2 red onions, diced
large handful of fresh flat-leaf
   parsley, chopped
2 Tbs. oyster sauce
2 Tbs. ketchup
1 egg yolk

'THE ROAST'

I've loved roast rib of beef ever since I was a child, not just because it smells so amazing when it is cooking. It is simply delicious, and arguably makes the best gravy of any roast meat. Just thinking about it makes me smile.

Roasting a rib of beef can be straightforward, but so many of us get it wrong. I hope the notes here will be a guide to success.

A standing rib roast is a large hunk of meat attached to some bones. Each bone with its meat will serve at least two people (this is the French *côte de boeuf*—which looks like something from the Flintstones; see page 132). A whole seven-bone rib roast is a huge hunk, but wow, is it exciting! Weighing in at about 15 pounds, I think it should be the centerpiece of any holiday feast or celebration.

A good rib needs marbling—marbling is just fat that is naturally in the meat. It slowly disappears (or renders) as it cooks, keeping the beef moist. If there is no fat through the meat, the result will be a dry and tasteless disappointment and you will get little yield from it. To make carving easier, choose a bone-in rib-eye roast, and be sure that the chine bone (which is actually the vertebrae) has been removed.

I salt the fat 12 hours before the roast goes into the oven, because I like the fat to be crisp. To do this, place the rib on the work surface so the fat is on top. Cut a criss-cross pattern in the fat with a sharp knife, being careful to cut only into the fat, not the meat. Make a 50/50 mixture of chopped fresh rosemary and salt and add a generous amount of pepper. Rub a handful of this seasoning over the fat, then turn the roast over and rub it into the rib bones and meat. Put the roast in the refrigerator, have a glass of red, and go to bed.

The next day, heat the oven to 350°F. For each rib bone (or about 3 pounds) I allow about 45 minutes cooking time. So a five-bone roast will take about 3¾ hours—you will get a well-done outside, medium just inside, then medium rare meat, and then, at the center, rare beef. After cooking, the beef must be left to rest for at least 20 minutes before it is carved. Put it on a board with the fat facing the carver and the bow of the bone pointing away.

I always roast some potatoes with the beef, putting them into the roasting pan with the beef about 1 hour and 20 minutes before the end of the cooking time. When they're done you can take them out and keep them warm in a serving dish, then use the beef drippings to make Yorkshire puddings (see page 156).

After the beef has been removed to rest, you'll be left with a roasting pan containing lots of tasty bits. Now it's time to make the gravy. My grandma's gravy recipe is very special to me. From the age of six, I stood on a stool and helped to make it; I loved stirring it while it was bubbling away.

You will need a little fat to get this gravy right, so when pouring off the drippings, keep about a tablespoon in the roasting pan. Set the pan over low heat. Sprinkle in about 2 tablespoons of flour and stir really well—the flour will become like brown bread crumbs.

Add a little salt, turn the heat up to medium, and pour in 1 cup water (cold is fine). Keep stirring—as the heat builds, the lumps will disappear and, once boiling, the gravy will get thick. Add some more water and boil again, stirring, to thicken. Then add more water and boil until thick. Finally, add some more water and boil until the gravy is the thickness you like.

Taste the gravy now—I bet you an Australian dollar that it does not need seasoning and it will be the best you have ever tried. It takes time but, boy, it is good.

Tip The bones in a roast conduct the heat and therefore help to cook it more evenly than a boneless roast. They also prevent shrinkage, so your yield is far better when cooking a bone-in roast. If you are going to cook a boneless roast, first sear it well on the stovetop before roasting: Rub it all over with oil, salt, and pepper, then place in a heavy skillet over high heat and turn so that it is well-colored on all sides.

'MY CHRISTMAS ROAST BEEF WITH MUSTARD CRUST'

5-bone beef rib roast, weighing
   about 11 lb., trimmed and
   chine bone removed
½ cup vegetable oil
salt and pepper
4 carrots, peeled and halved

mustard crust
4 Tbs. (½ stick) butter
2 large onions, diced
5 cups fresh white bread crumbs
1 heaped cup whole grain or
   other mustard
3 eggs
scant 1 cup water

You can use any type of mustard for this recipe. I like the speckled effect and flavor of wholegrain. If you prefer to use English mustard, be careful not to add too much as it is very hot.

Well before cooking, remove the beef from the refrigerator to let it come up to room temperature. Score the fat on the top of the roast well. Rub the roast all over with oil, then season with salt and pepper.

Heat the oven to 425°F.

To make the crust (which can be done the day before), heat the butter in a pan and sweat the onions until tender but not colored. Transfer them to a big bowl and add the bread crumbs, mustard, eggs, and water. Stir well to make a paste.

Spread the paste evenly over the beef, leaving the ends uncovered. Cover the crust with a sheet of well-greased foil. Place the carrots in a large roasting pan and set the beef on them. Roast for 2½ hours, removing the foil for the final hour. When done, take the beef from the oven and let it rest for 20 minutes while you make a gravy (recipes on pages 33 and 153).

'RED CABBAGE'

5 thick slices bacon, chopped

7 Tbs. butter

2 heads red cabbage, cored
and sliced

4 Granny Smith apples, peeled,
cored, and sliced

⅔ cup raisins

pared rind of ½ orange,
chopped

2 cinnamon sticks

1 cup packed brown sugar

salt and pepper

1¼ cups red wine

¼ cup red-wine vinegar

Place a Dutch oven over high heat. Add the bacon and fry until slightly colored, then remove and set aside.

Pour off most of the bacon fat from the pot, then add the butter and melt it. Lay one-quarter of the cabbage over the bottom. Top with one-quarter of the apples and raisins, plus some bacon, orange rind, cinnamon, and brown sugar. Season with salt and pepper. Repeat the layers until all the ingredients are used.

Set the pot over high heat and add the wine and vinegar. Bring to a boil and cook briskly for 3–4 minutes. Cover tightly, reduce the heat, and cook gently until the cabbage is tender, 1–2 hours. Do not stir the cabbage at any stage, but check the liquid level every 20 minutes or so to be sure that it does not evaporate too quickly. If it does, add more water.

'YORKSHIRE PUDDINGS'

8 eggs

2½ cups milk

½ tsp. salt

3⅓ cups all-purpose flour

3 Tbs. beef drippings

Heat the oven to 425°F. Beat the eggs with the milk and salt. Sift the flour twice to aerate it, then beat the flour into the milk mixture to make a batter. You can strain the batter, if desired.

Place a 12-cup muffin pan in the oven to heat, then add some drippings to each indentation and heat until the fat is smoking.

Now, take care as the fat is very hot. Ladle some of the batter into each of the cups so it is nearly full. Return the pan to the oven. Reduce the heat to 400°F and bake for 15 minutes.

'THE BEST ROASTED POTATOES'

20 large potatoes
1 cup beef drippings or lard

Many of us have been merrily popping potatoes into the oven on a high heat with a little oil for years and doing fine. In fact, I was one of those people—until I found out there was a way I could get a crisper potato, and much quicker!

Heat the oven to 425°F. Peel the potatoes and cut them in half, or into quarters if they are huge. Put them in a pot of boiling water and cook over high heat for 5 minutes.

Drain well. Put the potatoes back in the pot over low heat to dry them out, shaking the pot—but not too vigorously or the potatoes will be damaged.

Heat the drippings in a large baking dish in the oven for at least 10 minutes so it's really hot. Add the potatoes and turn to coat them in the fat. Place in the oven and roast for 20 minutes. Turn the potatoes over and continue roasting until they are tender, golden brown, and crisp, about 40 minutes longer. Drain off the fat and serve immediately.

'CLASSIC BEEF WELLINGTON WITH HONEY PARSNIPS'

½ oz. dried porcini
2–3-lb. center-cut tenderloin
    roast, trimmed
salt and pepper
3 Tbs. butter
2 shallots, chopped
2 garlic cloves, chopped
8 oz. cremini mushrooms,
    finely chopped
2 tsp. chopped fresh thyme
6 oz. chicken liver pâté
6 oz. prosciutto, sliced
all-purpose flour for dusting
1 package puff pastry, about 1 lb.
1 egg, beaten

honey parsnips

2 lb. parsnips, peeled
2 Tbs. vegetable oil
3 Tbs. butter
2 Tbs. honey

I don't care what anyone says—beef Wellington is the holy grail to any carnivore. Its reputation has suffered because it has so often been made badly for big catered events. This is a shame because it really is good. Although the recipe here is for six to eight people, four could devour it with no trouble at all.

Put the dried porcini in a heatproof bowl and cover with ½ cup boiling water. Let soak for 30 minutes, then drain, reserving the liquid. Chop the porcini, and set them and the liquid aside.

Season the beef all over with salt and pepper. Melt half the butter in a heavy skillet over medium heat. When foaming, put the beef in the pan and brown all over for 4–5 minutes, taking care not to burn the butter. Put the beef on a plate and set aside to cool.

Melt the remaining butter in a separate frying pan. Add the shallots and cook for 1 minute. Add the porcini and garlic, then the reserved porcini liquid and the cremini mushrooms. Increase the heat and cook until the mushroom mixture is dry. Season with salt and pepper and add the thyme, then set aside to cool.

Put the pâté in a bowl and beat until smooth. Add the mushroom mixture and stir well. Adjust the seasoning as necessary.

Use a metal spatula to spread half the mushroom mixture evenly over one side of the beef. Lay a sheet of plastic wrap on the work surface and arrange half of the prosciutto on it so that the slices overlap. Place the beef mushroom-side down on the prosciutto. Spread the remaining mushroom mixture over the beef. Wrap the rest of the prosciutto slices, overlapped, over the top. Wrap the whole thing in the plastic wrap and refrigerate.

Heat the oven to 425°F. Take about one-third of the puff pastry from the package and roll it out to a rectangle ⅛ inch thick and

1 inch larger than the base of the roast. Transfer to a baking sheet. Prick well with a fork and bake until brown and crisp, 12–15 minutes. Let the pastry cool, then trim it to the size of the roast.

Take the beef from the refrigerator and unwrap it. Brush the beef all over with some of the beaten egg, then place it on the pastry base.

Roll out the remaining pastry to a rectangle about 12 by 14 inches. Use this to cover the beef, tucking the sides under the base and sealing the edges. Brush with the rest of the beaten egg. Place the Wellington on a baking sheet. Bake for 40 minutes for rare to medium rare beef, and 45 minutes for medium.

Meanwhile, halve the parsnips lengthwise; if very large, cut them into quarters. Trim out any woody centers. Place a roasting pan over high heat and add the oil and butter. Fry the parsnips until golden brown on all sides, then transfer to the oven and roast for 20 minutes, turning occasionally.

Take the parsnips from the oven. Drizzle the honey over them and stir carefully until they are well coated. Continue roasting for about 5 minutes.

Remove the Wellington from the oven and let it stand for about 10 minutes before slicing. Put the parsnips in a large serving dish and spoon some of the honey glaze over the top to finish.

'GROUND BEEF WELLINGTON'

2 lb. ground sirloin

8 oz. onions, diced

handful of chopped fresh sage leaves

handful of chopped fresh parsley

2 garlic cloves, crushed

salt and pepper

6 Tbs. tomato paste

3 eggs

10 oz. puff pastry

4 oz. pâté of your choice

I had to include this recipe. When I was a kid we could not afford tenderloin to make Beef Wellington, so my grandma made this instead. It is really a meatloaf in puff pastry. I still like it a lot. If you have picky kids, leave out the pâté. You can also use the meat mixture to make a regular meatloaf—just put it in a loaf pan and bake for 40 minutes or so.

Mix the beef with the onions, herbs, garlic, and lots of seasoning. In a bowl, stir the tomato paste with ½ cup water, then whisk in two of the eggs. Add the egg mixture to the beef and beat with an electric mixer for 5 minutes.

Heat the oven to 400°F. Shape the meat into a large sausage, place in a roasting pan, and cook in the oven for 20 minutes. Strain off and reserve the pan juices, and set them and the meat aside to cool.

Roll out the pastry to a large rectangle about ⅛ inch thick. Beat the remaining egg with a little water and brush over the top of the pastry. Place the meat in the middle and roll the pastry over the meat to enclose it. Cover with the pâté.

Place on a baking sheet and bake for 30 minutes. Shortly before serving, reheat the pan juices to serve with the Wellington, plus some mashed potatoes and ketchup.

'VIETNAMESE GRILLED STEAK'

4 "minute" steaks
2 scallions, shredded
1 tsp. sesame seeds

sauce

1 Tbs. rice vinegar
1 fresh red chile, chopped
5 tsp. fish sauce
juice of 1 lime
1 carrot, peeled and grated
1 garlic clove, chopped
1 knob fresh ginger, peeled
  and chopped
2½ Tbs. sugar

garnish

1 Thai shallot, chopped
1 garlic clove, chopped
1 Tbs. sugar
1 tsp. fish sauce
ground pepper
12 fresh mint leaves, chopped
handful of fresh Thai basil
handful of chopped fresh
  cilantro
2 yard-long beans, chopped

The minute steak is simply that—a steak that has been bashed until thin so it takes just a minute or so to cook. I prefer to use boneless sirloin as it has great flavor, but it's up to you. As with all steak cooking, the secret lies in the heat of the skillet, grill pan, or coals. You must get them really hot, and the oil must go on the steak and not on the pan or grill.

To make the sauce, heat the vinegar in a saucepan and add the chopped chile. Let cool slightly, then add the fish sauce, lime juice, carrot, garlic, and ginger. Add the sugar and 1½ cups water and stir until the sugar has dissolved. Set aside.

Combine all the ingredients for the garnish in a bowl, then toss with a little of the sauce. Spread on serving plates.

Fry, pan-grill, or grill the steaks for about 30 seconds on each side, then place on top of the vegetable garnish. Sprinkle the scallions and sesame seeds on top before serving with the rest of the sauce.

'SIRLOIN ROAST WITH OYSTER SAUCE & GINGER'

4-lb. boneless sirloin roast, with
its layer of fat on
2 tsp. Chinese five-spice powder
1 tsp. sugar
salt and pepper
vegetable oil

sauce

1¼ cups chicken stock
1 garlic clove
5 Tbs. Chinese oyster sauce
3 scallions
1 thumb-sized piece fresh
ginger, peeled and skin
reserved
½ bunch of fresh cilantro

The night before, score the fat on the sirloin roast in a criss-cross pattern. Mix together the five-spice powder, sugar, a heaped teaspoon of ground pepper, and a generous amount of salt. Rub this into the fat and leave overnight.

Next day, when ready to cook, heat the oven to 400°F. Take some oil and rub it forcefully all over the meat. Set a ridged cast-iron grill pan or broiler pan over high heat and leave it for about 10 minutes to get really hot.

Place the meat fat-side down in the pan and leave to shimmer. The fat will start to melt and the spices start to cook. Don't touch it. If you have scored the fat well you have no worries at all. After 5 minutes, turn the meat over and transfer it to the oven. Roast for 25 minutes. Remove from the oven and let rest, or even cool for serving later.

Meanwhile, combine the stock, garlic, and oyster sauce in a large saucepan along with the trimmings from the scallions, the ginger peel, and the stems from the cilantro (reserve the leaves). Bring to a boil, then remove from the heat and let infuse for 5 minutes.

Cut the ginger into the thinnest slices and those slice into the thinnest strips. Slice the scallions, keeping the white portion separate from the green. Mix the scallion greens with the cilantro leaves and set aside for garnishing.

Strain the flavorings from the stock and return the liquid to the pan. Bring back to a boil and add the shredded ginger and the white parts of the scallions. Take off the heat immediately.

Sauce made. Beef cooked. Serve up.

Tip This flavored stock is also good for cooking Asian vegetables, such as bok choy, choy sum, and Chinese broccoli, all of which taste best when served hot.

'RIB ROAST WITH HORSERADISH BREAD PUDDING'

6-lb. boneless rib roast, rolled and tied

4 tsp. salt

2 tsp. ground pepper

$\frac{2}{3}$ cup vegetable oil or beef drippings

20 large potatoes, peeled and halved

horseradish bread puddings

1 small loaf white bread

butter for greasing

4 eggs

$\frac{1}{2}$ cup sour cream

$\frac{1}{2}$ cup creamed horseradish (recipe on page 130)

1 cup chicken stock

salt and pepper

The accompaniment for the beef is the same as a bread pudding—but savory, not sweet. It is very delicious but must be crisp on top.

Heat the oven to 400°F. Rub the roast with salt and pepper and then with at least 4 tablespoons of vegetable oil. Put the rest of the oil in a roasting pan and heat in the oven for 10 minutes.

Add the potatoes to the roasting pan and place the beef in the center. Turn the beef once and shake the potatoes so they are covered with oil. Return the roasting pan to the oven and roast, without opening the oven door, for 30 minutes.

Meanwhile, take the crusts off the loaf of bread. Slice the bread and cut each slice into triangles. Butter a baking dish.

Mix together the eggs, sour cream, horseradish, stock, and some salt and pepper. Overlap the bread triangles in the dish with the points sticking up, then pour the egg mixture over the bread. Place in the oven to bake alongside the beef until crisp and golden brown, about 40 minutes.

Take out the beef when it is cooked and let it rest while you use the pan juices to make a gravy (recipes on pages 33 and 153). Serve the beef with the potatoes, pudding, and gravy, plus some green beans and extra creamed horseradish.

CORNED BEEF
BRESAOLA & PASTRAMI

Salting and smoking are traditional techniques devised to cope with seasonal gluts of fresh meat. Cattle would feed on grass all summer, and then, as the cold came, fatten up on the grain that was left after harvest. Once the cattle were slaughtered, the fresh meat had to be eaten right away or it would spoil. The seafaring Dutch did a swap for Manhattan in order to secure supplies of nutmeg, a natural preservative used in curing, thus insuring their ships had good supplies of preserved meat. For me, salting and curing a piece of beef like brisket is a real treat. Boiled with carrots and served hot with mustard and parsley sauce, it is perfect comfort food. At the same time, a simple corned beef or pastrami sandwich, with hot mustard and a dill pickle, is also a great treat.

'CORNED BEEF'

6½–8½ lb. piece boneless
   brisket, top round, or bottom
   round, trimmed of any fat
4½ quarts boiling water
2½ lb. sea salt
3 cups packed dark brown sugar
½ cup coriander seeds
24 juniper berries
12 black peppercorns
12 allspice berries
4 whole cloves
2 cardamom pods
6 cups ice-cold water
6 bay leaves

Making corned beef is not something many of us will do, but should you want to try, this is how to go about it. The thickness of the beef will determine how long it stays in the brine: a whole top round roast, which will be round like a soccer ball, will take 2 weeks, but a small book-shaped brisket takes about 4 days.

Under no circumstances should the meat have bone in, on, or near it, as this will rot rather than pickle. Have the boiling water ready in a pot. Add the salt and sugar and bring back to a boil.

Meanwhile, heat a large frying pan until almost smoking and throw in all the spices. Take off the heat and let the spices toast, shaking the pan a few times so they toast evenly. Tie the spices in a piece of cheesecloth or an old dishtowel, then drop into the boiling water. Keep the water boiling for 15 minutes to dissolve the salt and sugar and make the liquid very salty. Then remove from the heat, pour in the cold water, and let cool.

Add the meat and bay leaves to the brine, making sure the meat is completely immersed, and cover tightly. Leave in the refrigerator for the time needed (see above). You can turn the meat every so often, but try just to let it bob about in the liquid.

Once cured, it can be kept for a few days in the refrigerator.

'CORNED BEEF, PEASE PUDDING & STUFF'

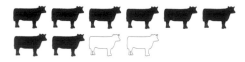

pease pudding
1 cup whole dried peas

1 tsp. baking soda

4 Tbs. (½ stick) butter

salt and pepper

1 egg

corned beef
4½ lb. corned beef (recipe on
  page 166)

2 large onions, peeled and
  halved

2 large carrots, peeled and
  halved

1 celery rib

12 black peppercorns

2 bay leaves

2 parsley stems

mustard sauce
4 Tbs. (½ stick) butter

¼ cup all-purpose flour

2½ cups milk

2 Tbs. German mustard

potatoes
8–12 large potatoes, peeled
  and halved

butter

The great thing about large hunks of preserved meat is that you can eat them over a period of time. In the modern world there's a tendency for people to look at recipes that only last one meal, when the real way to save time in the kitchen is to cook dishes that last three or four meals. Remember the beef has already been cooked by the salting process, so all you are really doing here is getting it hot.

The night before serving, soak the peas in lots of water. The next day, drain off the water and rinse the peas three times. Then put them in a saucepan, cover with water, and add the baking soda, stirring well. Bring to a boil and cook until tender, about 1 hour, replenishing the water so the peas are always covered.

While the peas are cooking, start the beef. Put it into a large pot with the vegetables, peppercorns, bay leaves, and parsley stems. Cover with water and bring to a rolling simmer. Cook for at least 2 hours, periodically replenishing the water.

Once the peas are cooked, put them in a food processor with the butter, lots of salt and pepper, and a little of their cooking liquid. Blend until nearly smooth, then add the egg and mix well. Taste and adjust the seasoning, if necessary.

Take a dishtowel or (something I like to use) an old, clean pillow case and lay it in a bowl. Spoon the pea mush into the middle, then tie it up in a bundle with string. Put the whole thing in the pot with the beef as it continues cooking.

To make the sauce, melt the butter over low heat. Stir in the flour to make a roux. Add the milk, stirring well until smooth. Bring to a boil, then add the mustard and a little salt and remove from the heat. I like to blend the sauce to aerate it and make it really silky

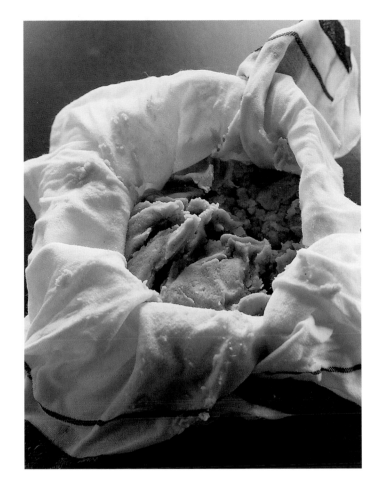

—you can do this with a hand-held blender, a regular blender, or a food processor. Alternatively, just beat it really hard or push it through a strainer. Return the sauce to the pan and reheat it, adding a little of the cooking liquid from the corned beef.

About 20 minutes before the beef will be ready, put the potatoes in a pan of cold water with some salt. Add some of the cooking liquid from the beef and bring to a boil. Cook until tender, about 20 minutes. Drain the potatoes. Put them in a bowl with a generous amount of butter and keep warm while you get everything else ready to serve.

To serve, slice the corned beef. Open the pease pudding and serve it in spoonfuls with the beef, potatoes, and mustard sauce.

'BREAD SAUCE'

2 cups milk

1 medium onion, peeled and halved

6 black peppercorns

2 whole cloves

1 small blade mace, or a pinch of grated nutmeg

flaked sea salt

2 cups fresh white bread crumbs

2 Tbs. butter

It wasn't until I landed on the shores of Great Britain that I discovered bread sauce. It may be new to you, too. Served with all sorts of salted meats, poultry, and game, it is truly delicious.

Put the milk in a saucepan and add the onion, peppercorns, cloves, mace or nutmeg, and some salt. Set the pan over medium heat and heat the milk to scalding point. Cook for 5 minutes, then remove the pan from the heat and let infuse for at least 15 minutes, but preferably 1 hour.

Take a clean saucepan and put the bread crumbs in it. Pour the infused milk through a strainer into the pan, then let soak for 5 minutes. Set the pan over medium heat and cook the sauce gently for 10 minutes, stirring often.

Stir in the butter. The sauce should be thick—a bit like oatmeal. If it is too thick, add a little more milk; if too thin, continue cooking until enough liquid has evaporated and the sauce has the desired consistency.

'PARSLEY SAUCE'

4 Tbs. (½ stick) butter

¼ cup all-purpose flour

1 cup milk

1 cup broth from cooking corned beef (recipe on page 168)

1 Tbs. English mustard powder

salt and pepper

handful of fresh parsley, stems trimmed off

Another great sauce to serve with corned beef.

In a saucepan, melt the butter, then stir in the flour and cook over low heat for 2 minutes.

Mix the milk and broth, add the mustard, and stir to dissolve. Season with salt and pepper as necessary. Gradually add the liquid to the butter and flour roux, stirring constantly to prevent lumps. Bring to a boil and cook for 5 minutes.

Rip up the parsley and add. Using a hand-held blender (or a blender or food processor), pulse until the sauce turns green. Pour the sauce over your corned beef and vegetables.

'CORNED BEEF HASH, SPINACH & FRIED EGGS'

8 oz. corned beef
3 large baked potatoes, peeled
salt and pepper
½ cup (1 stick) butter
4 eggs
4 oz. baby spinach leaves
   (about 1 cup)

For brunch, it doesn't get much better than this–equal amounts of shredded corned beef and potatoes fried in butter! You can make this dish by cooking it in little pans and serving with poached eggs, or you can use one big pan and serve it scooped out with fried eggs.

Shred the corned beef and your peeled baked potatoes using the coarse side of a cheese grater. Mix the two together. Season with lots of pepper and maybe some salt, then knead the mixture really well.

Drop half the butter into a nonstick frying pan and, as it starts to melt, add half of the hash mixture. Give it a stir and let it color on the bottom, then give another stir and let it color some more. Stir again so that it is all hot. Press down on the hash so it flattens into a thick cake.

Meanwhile, poach or fry the eggs.

Cover the hash with half the spinach leaves. Let it cook for a few minutes, then fold one half of the hash over like an omelet and flip it out onto a plate. Keep it warm while you repeat the cooking process with the rest of the hash mixture. Cut each batch in half and serve with the eggs.

'CORNED BEEF SANDWICH, PICKLES & MUSTARD MAYONNAISE'

2 thick slices soft rye bread
mayonnaise
Dijon mustard
hot corned beef
big dill pickle

In the Jewish tradition, you can't eat dairy products and beef together, which is why the bread for this sandwich is spread with mayo instead of butter.

Make your sandwich in the usual way, spreading the bread with the mayonnaise and then adding a stripe of mustard.

Slice the hot corned beef—not too thick—and pile it onto the bread. You can then either slice the pickle and put it inside the sandwich, or serve it on the side—or both.

'BRESAOLA'

8½-lb. boneless top round roast

marinade

1½ lb. coarse sea salt
  (about 5 cups)
1 bottle cheap red wine
1 bottle cheap white wine
large bunch of fresh rosemary
12 bay leaves
24 whole cloves
3 garlic cloves, crushed
40 black peppercorns
12 dried red chiles
4 strips orange peel

For this classic Italian cured beef, the meat is first marinated and then hung to dry, which takes 40 days. You can buy bresaola from Italian markets, to serve with the following dishes, but why not try preserving it yourself? This recipe will give you three or four generous pieces that will last a family for 6 months. If you want to make less, simply reduce the volume of ingredients to suit 2 pounds or so of beef—it's not really worth making less than this.

Trim the beef, removing the fat and sinews so that you have a number of nuggets of meat rather than one big hunk. Combine all the ingredients for the marinade in a large non-reactive dish that is big enough to hold all the meat comfortably. Add the meat, cover, and leave for 2 weeks in the back of the refrigerator.

At the end of this time, cut squares of cheesecloth big enough to wrap each hunk of meat. Take the meat from the marinade and wrap up each piece, then tie it into a bundle with some string. Hang the meat somewhere cool that allows the air to circulate, a dry basement would be ideal, and let dry for 2 weeks. Check every so often that the bundles of beef are not touching each other, otherwise the air won't circulate freely around them.

To serve the bresaola, slice it very thinly. Sprinkle with olive oil and season with pepper and chives. Garnish with wedges of lemon and eat with chunks of bread.

'BRESAOLA WITH CELERY ROOT & MUSTARD DRESSING'

1 large head celery root

large handful of chopped fresh
  flat-leaf parsley

32 slices bresaola

4 tsp. olive oil

4 lemon wedges

dressing

2 Tbs. Dijon mustard

1 Tbs. champagne vinegar

½ Tbs. sugar

2 Tbs. vegetable oil

½ Tbs. hazelnut oil

½ cup light cream

Celeri rémoulade is a very quick, classic French salad to serve with cured meats and fish. This is good with a soft-cooked egg on top, too.

Make the dressing first. In a bowl, whisk together the mustard, vinegar, sugar, and both oils until combined. Add the cream and whisk gently for 20 seconds just to incorporate—if you beat it too much it will thicken and separate.

Peel and slice the celery root, then cut it into thin strips—as thin as linguine. Alternatively, you can shred it on a mandoline. Gently mix the dressing with the celery root and parsley.

Lay the bresaola out on four serving plates. Wind the celery root strips around a fork, as if you were eating spaghetti, and place them in the center of the bresaola. Sprinkle each plate with olive oil and serve with a wedge of lemon.

'BRESAOLA & MOZZARELLA PIZZA'

tomato sauce
¼ cup olive oil
1 onion, diced
1 garlic clove, crushed
1 tsp. flaked sea salt
1 tsp. ground black pepper
28-oz. can crushed tomatoes

dough
1 cup warm water
1 cake compressed fresh yeast
½ tsp sugar
3 cups Italian "oo" (*doppio zero*)
   pasta flour, plus extra
   for dusting
1 tsp. salt
1 Tbs. olive oil, plus extra
   for greasing

topping
36 slices bresaola
8 oz. mozzarella, torn into pieces

I don't know anybody who doesn't like pizza. This is the quickest and best dough I know of to make a truly thin and crisp pizza base.

For the tomato sauce, heat the oil in a heavy-based pan over medium heat. Add the onion and cook for 3 minutes, stirring constantly. Add the garlic, salt, and pepper, and cook for another 2 minutes, then add the tomatoes and bring to a boil. Reduce the heat to a simmer and cook for about 20 minutes, stirring occasionally. Take the pan off the heat and let cool. (This recipe will give plenty of leftover sauce for another day.)

To make the dough, mix together the water, yeast, and sugar, and let sit for 10 minutes. Place half the flour in the bowl of an electric mixer fitted with a dough hook and pour in the liquid. Beat at medium speed for 10 minutes, then leave somewhere warm until foamy, about 10 minutes.

Add the rest of the flour, the salt, and olive oil and beat for 5 minutes. Put the dough in a well-oiled bowl, cover with a cloth, and let rise somewhere warm until the dough has doubled in size, about 30 minutes.

Slap the dough down and knead until soft but not too elastic, about 4 minutes. Separate into six equal pieces and roll each into a ball. Let rest for 10 minutes.

Heat the oven to its highest temperature and put two rimless baking sheets in the oven to get very hot. With a well-floured rolling pin, flatten each ball and roll it out as thinly as possible. Take the sheets from the oven, lightly oil them, and dust with a little flour. Lay the dough on the hot sheets. Spoon on a little of your tomato sauce, spreading it out. Scatter the bresaola and mozzarella over the top. Bake for about 10 minutes.

'BRESAOLA & ROASTED RED PEPPER SALAD'

3 large, red bell peppers
4 red onions, peeled
1 garlic clove, peeled
¼ cup olive oil, plus extra
  for serving
32–40 slices bresaola
4-oz. bouquet of watercress
2 oz. Parmesan cheese, shaved
black pepper

To make this really fast, you can cheat by buying a jar of roasted bell peppers. I like a bit of watercress in this salad, but you could use arugula instead. It doesn't need much else except hungry people to devour it.

Heat the oven to 400°F. Put the whole peppers, red onions, garlic clove, and olive oil in a roasting pan. Roast for 15 minutes, then turn the vegetables and roast for 20 minutes longer. The peppers should be dark on the outside. Remove them, place in a mixing bowl, and cover with plastic wrap. Roast the onions and garlic for 15 more minutes.

When the onions are done, set them aside to cool a little. Remove the plastic wrap from the peppers and cut them down the center, discarding the seeds and core. Peel off the skin, then cut the flesh into quarters and return it to the bowl with all the pepper juices. Pop the onions from their skins, cut them in quarters, and mix them with the peeled peppers and juice.

On a large plate, pile up all the remaining ingredients, mixing them with the roasted vegetables. Finish with a good grind of pepper and a trickle of olive oil, and serve with crusty bread.

ALSO GOOD WITH BRESAOLA: Olive oil and shaved truffles ☛ Arugula and buttered toast ☛ Dill pickles and mustard mayonnaise ☛ Watercress,

'BRESAOLA WITH ASPARAGUS VINAIGRETTE'

32 asparagus spears
salt
20 slices bresaola
handful of fresh chervil leaves

vinaigrette
7 fl. oz. extra-virgin olive oil
7 Tbs. red-wine vinegar
1 tsp. balsamic vinegar
1 tsp. Dijon mustard
salt and pepper

Asparagus spears have a tough base and a tender stem and tip. Near the base, where the white starts to turn to green, they will naturally snap. Break each one individually rather than cutting off the ends.

Fill a pot with cold water, add a generous teaspoon of salt, and bring to a boil. Tie the asparagus into three bundles with kitchen string—don't tie too tightly or it will damage the asparagus—and drop the bundles into the boiling water. Bring back to a boil and cook for 4 minutes—no longer or they will be floppy and the tips will disintegrate.

To make the vinaigrette, mix all the ingredients in a jar and shake it like mad. When the asparagus is cooked, dress it with some of the vinaigrette.

Lay the bresaola out on serving plates and drop the asparagus on top. Garnish with the chervil and drizzle the remaining vinaigrette over the bresaola before serving.

torn mozzarella ☛ Roasted tomatoes and shaved Parmesan ☛ Hot horseradish, and beets ☛ Shaved Romano and a fresh herb salad

'PASTRAMI'

corned beef, made with brisket
  (recipe on page 166)
⅓ cup table salt
2 Tbs. smoked paprika
1 cup coriander seeds
5 Tbs. packed brown sugar
2 Tbs. cracked black pepper
2 Tbs. yellow mustard seeds
8 oz. lapsang souchong tea
  leaves or other smoky black
  tea leaves (about 3 cups)
10 oz. wood chips for smoking

Pastrami is wonderful served simply with good bread, cornichons (tiny, tart pickled gherkins), and piccalilli (recipe on page 184), or used to make a sandwich (see page 185).

First you have to make corned beef, which will take at least 4 days. Once you are ready to proceed with making pastrami, use a mortar and pestle to crush the salt, smoked paprika, coriander seeds, sugar, pepper, and mustard seeds together. The mixture should just be crushed, not powdered.

Set up a smoker, or use a kettle barbecue that has a tight-fitting lid. Make a small fire out of very good quality wood and let it burn down to glowing coals. Mix the tea and wood chips together and place them on top of the glowing coals.

Rub the meat all over with the spice mixture and place on a flat rack in the smoker or barbecue. Cover with the lid and seal the whole thing with foil. Let the meat smoke for 2 hours. Open the smoker, turn the meat over, reseal, and smoke for 2 hours longer.

'PICCALILLI'

Makes 15 lb.

1 lb. table salt (about 2 cups)

5 ½ lb. zucchini

5 ½ lb. cauliflower

4 ½ lb. frozen pearl onions, thawed

2 ½ cups sugar

1 cup all-purpose flour

⅓ cup English mustard powder

¼ cup ground turmeric

1 ½ Tbs. ground ginger

2 quarts white-wine vinegar

This recipe makes a lot, but once in jars it will last for ages, and is great with all kinds of cold cuts.

Combine 4 ½ quarts of water and the salt in a very large pot and bring to a boil, stirring until all the salt has dissolved. Remove from the heat and let this brine cool.

Cut the zucchini into chunks the size of your thumbnail, and cut the cauliflower into tiny florets. Add the pearl onions, zucchini, and cauliflower to the brine. Cover the vegetables with a plate or a lid that will fit inside the pot, so they are submerged in the brine, and leave in a cool place for 24 hours.

Drain the brine from the vegetables and discard it, then rinse the vegetables briefly under cold water. Put them in a large bowl.

Combine the sugar, flour, mustard, turmeric, ginger, and vinegar in a pot and heat gently, stirring until thoroughly blended. Pour the spice mixture over the brined vegetables and mix very well. Spread out on trays and let cool. Pack the piccalilli into sterilized jars and seal.

'JOHN'S BIG TASTY PASTRAMI SANDWICH'

1¼-lb. round crusty Italian
    bread loaf

2 cups chopped green olives
    stuffed with pimientos

3 large garlic cloves, chopped

large handful of chopped fesh
    flat-leaf parsley

7 Tbs. olive oil

2 Tbs. white-wine vinegar

7 oz. canned artichoke hearts
    (about ½ can), drained
    and halved

8 oz. mozzarella, sliced

¾ cup chopped black or
    Kalamata olives

8 oz. pastrami, sliced

8 oz. Provolone or Jarlsberg
    cheese, sliced

1½ cups chopped roasted
    red bell peppers

This is actually a muffaletta, which is basically a big sandwich filled with lots of meat and cheese. It travels very well, so once at the spot of your picnic or family outing it can be cut to feed the hungry hordes. The roasted peppers can be made at home or you can use those bottled in oil or brine. This is both fun to make and fun to eat.

Cut the loaf in half horizontally and scoop out a little of the bread inside to make some room for the filling. Mix the green olives with the garlic, parsley, olive oil, and vinegar.

Spoon half the olive mixture into the bottom of the loaf, followed by all the artichokes and sliced mozzarella, then the black olives and some pastrami. Add the Provolone or Jarlsberg, followed by the rest of the green olives, then the roasted peppers. Top with the last of the pastrami.

Place the top half of the loaf in place, tucking in all the filling. Wrap with a dishtowel to secure the two halves together, insuring that nothing can leak out the sides, then add a second layer of towel.

Turn the loaf upside down and put it in the refrigerator with a few plates stacked on top to weight it down and compress the bread into the filling. Leave for 2 hours. Eat within a day, cutting the loaf into wedges to serve.

VEAL

I love beef in all its guises and that includes veal. Veal is a by-product of the dairy industry—male dairy animals don't produce milk and don't grow into great beef cattle, but they do make great veal. In Europe—particularly Italy, France, and Germany—veal has always been much used in cooking. In Britain and the United States, however, much less veal is eaten, mainly because of objections to rearing methods. These have changed, and today veal can be enjoyed with a clear conscience. Pale bob veal is from milk-fed calves; veal from "special-fed" calves is creamy pink and has a firm, velvety texture; grain-fed calves produce meat that is darker pink and slightly stronger in flavor. Baby beef comes from older animals. It is lighter in color, more tender, and leaner than beef, but stronger in flavor and coarser than veal.

'HOW TO COOK VEAL CHOPS'

Plainly cooked veal chops are wonderful—soft, sweet, and delicious. Cooking them is not difficult. You just need to trust yourself and be confident. You can fry or pan-grill them, and the following rules apply to both methods. Remember that a veal chop is a chop, a chop has a bone in it, and that bone is big. Given plenty of time and constant heat, the bone will conduct heat right down to the T-junction, but it needs a constant, not-too-hot heat.

Heat your pan and turn the oven on to 375°F. As with a good steak, oil the meat, not the pan, then season it with salt and pepper. Lay the chop on the pan and let it sizzle, really sizzle, for 2 minutes before turning it. (If the meat is stuck to the pan, it is not ready to turn, which means the pan was not hot enough.)

Once you've turned it, cook for another 2 minutes. Turn again, then put the pan in the oven to roast for 8 minutes. Take it out of the oven and turn the chop once more, then let rest in the pan off the heat for 3 minutes.

The juice that will be left in the pan is delicious, so after resting you can take the chop out, place the pan back on the heat, and add a lump of butter the size of your thumb. Let it melt with the pan juices and, when it starts to bubble, squeeze in the juice of half a lemon. Pour over the chop and serve.

'JOHN'S SOFT POLENTA'

1¼ cups milk

½ tsp. salt

¼ tsp. pepper

1 garlic clove, crushed

1 cup instant polenta

½ cup heavy cream

3 Tbs. freshly grated Parmesan cheese

¼ cup mascarpone

Put the milk in a large saucepan with the salt, pepper, garlic, and 1 cup water and bring to a rolling boil. Sprinkle in the polenta, stirring all the time with a wooden spoon, and keep stirring until the mixture returns to a boil. Cook over very low heat for about 45 minutes, stirring often and in one direction only, otherwise you will let the evil spirits escape.

Add the cream and Parmesan and stir well until the cheese has melted into the polenta. Remove the pan from the heat and mix in the mascarpone.

To serve, take a big spoonful of the soft, hot polenta and drop onto a warmed plate. Sit your veal chop on the polenta and pour any pan juices over. Serve with half a lemon each. Simple.

Tip Though it may sound a bit strange, cooking "instant" polenta quickly according to the packet instructions simply does not work for this particular dish. While it might take a bit longer, applying the very slow cooking method described above will help achieve the soft, creamy texture that makes this polenta extra special.

'GINGER SPICED CHICKPEAS'

1 cup dried chickpeas, or 3 cups
  canned chickpeas

7 Tbs. vegetable oil

2 oz. fresh ginger, peeled and
  pounded to a paste

1 Tbs. cayenne pepper, or to
  taste (optional)

1 Tbs. ground cumin

1 Tbs. ground coriander

2 tsp. salt

14-oz. can crushed tomatoes

salt and pepper

handful of fresh cilantro,
  chopped

I first ate a dish similar to this in a little café in Sydney, Australia. The only cooking medium they had was two burners on a stove and a microwave, but the food was always fabulous. The chickpeas were originally served with chicken, but I now love them with veal chops.

Chickpeas are a great alternative to starchy foods like potatoes or pasta, and this dish can be made a day, or even a few days, in advance and kept in the refrigerator, where the flavor will improve. The kick from the cayenne pepper is optional, although I think it adds to the overall dish, so please give it a try. You can reduce or increase the quantity, depending on how hot you like your food.

If you are using dried chickpeas, soak them in water overnight. The next day, bring to a boil in plenty of fresh water—without salt. Cook until tender, about 2 hours. Drain the chickpeas, reserving 1¼ cups of the cooking liquid. If using canned chickpeas, drain them, reserving the liquid from the can. Add enough water to the liquid to make 1¼ cups.

Place a heavy, deep frying pan or sauté pan over medium heat and add the oil. Let it heat for 2 minutes, then throw in the ginger, spices, and salt. Cook, stirring constantly, until lightly browned, 2–3 minutes. Add the chickpeas, tomatoes, and reserved chickpea cooking liquid. Increase the heat, bring to a boil, and cook for 10 minutes.

Remove the pan from the heat. Add the chopped cilantro and stir well. Taste and adjust the seasoning as necessary, then serve alongside your veal chops. If you make the chickpeas in advance and let them cool, remember to reheat gently, covered, in the microwave before serving.

'FAVA BEAN MASH WITH ROMANO'

2 cups shelled fresh fava beans,
   or frozen lima beans
3 Tbs. mascarpone
½ cup grated Romano cheese
salt and pepper

This is a terrific accompaniment to veal. The flavor is full and the consistency creamy. It is also great served with a piece of fresh fish and a wedge of lemon.

Bring a large pot of water to a boil. Add the fava beans and cook for 5 minutes, then drain and cool under cold running water.

Take each bean and squeeze one end so that the inner bean pops out from the tough skin (fun to do with the kids).

Heat the mascarpone in a small, heavy saucepan. Add the Romano and then the beans and stir well. Season with salt and pepper to taste. Place the bean mixture in a blender and pulse to a rough paste.

ALSO GOOD WITH VEAL CHOPS: Mashed potato and cèpes bordelaise sauce and straw potatoes 🐄 Mustard and fries 🐄 Broiled mushrooms,

'PAN-GRILLED VEAL CHOPS WITH PEAS, ARTICHOKES, & BACON'

7 Tbs. extra-virgin olive oil

1 large shallot, diced

1 garlic clove, minced

4 thick bacon slices, diced

1¼ cups frozen green peas

4 artichoke hearts in oil, chopped

salt and pepper

4 veal loin chops

a little fresh thyme, leaves picked from stems

4 Tbs. (½ stick) butter

Heat the olive oil slowly in a saucepan or frying pan. Add the shallot and garlic and cook very gently for 10 minutes, stirring occasionally. Add the bacon and cook for 5 minutes longer. Drain off the excess fat and keep it for cooking the chops. Stir the peas into the pan and then the artichokes. Season to taste with salt and pepper and set aside at room temperature.

Heat a ridged cast-iron grill pan or broiler pan until it is very hot. Rub the veal chops with the reserved fat and season well with salt and pepper. Heat the oven to 400°F.

Pan-grill the chops for 2–3 minutes on each side to give them plenty of color—they are best if a little charred. Transfer the pan to the oven to continue cooking for 3–4 minutes for medium-rare. Let the chops rest for a few minutes while you add the thyme and butter to the pan. When sizzling, pour over the chops and serve with the peas, artichokes, and bacon.

🐄 Fried potatoes with capers and lemon 🐄 Béarnaise sauce chopped parsley, and olive oil 🐄 Fried egg and tomato sauce

'ROAST VEAL RUMP WITH SAUCE SOUBISE'

1 boneless veal rump, sirloin,
  or round roast, about 3 lb.
7 Tbs. olive oil
salt and pepper
1 leek
3 carrots
small bunch of fresh rosemary
¾ cup white wine

sauce soubise
4 small onions
1 bay leaf
1 tsp. vinegar
1½ Tbs. butter
2 Tbs. all-purpose flour
1 cup milk
¼ cup cream
salt and white pepper

A real blast from the past, this recipe has a great basic pot-roasting method that can be used for most meats, but especially those cuts that would dry out if simply roasted. The sauce is a classic French white onion sauce. Use small onions rather than large ones, because the bigger they are, the sweeter they get.

Heat the oven to 400°F. Rub the veal with the oil, then season with lots of salt and pepper. Cut up the leek and carrots and put them in the bottom of a Dutch oven. Set the veal on top. Add the rosemary and then the wine and a little water. Cover the Dutch oven and set over high heat. Once the liquid is boiling, transfer to the oven and cook for 50 minutes.

Raise the heat to 425°F. Remove the lid from the Dutch oven and continue cooking the veal for 20 minutes.

Meanwhile, make the sauce. Peel and slice the onions, then put them in a large, heavy saucepan with the bay leaf, vinegar, butter, and 1 cup of water. Bring to a boil over high heat and cook the onions, boiling off the water so they are left in some butter. Once the water has all evaporated, the butter will start to sizzle, but don't let the onions brown.

Stir in the flour and then the milk. Bring to a boil, stirring, then take the pan off the heat. Transfer the sauce to a food processor and blend until smooth. Pour into a clean saucepan and bring to a simmer. Add the cream, then taste and adjust the seasoning as needed. Serve with the veal and green peas.

'VEAL SCALOPPINE WITH LEMON'

4 veal cutlets, about 4 oz. each
¼ cup vegetable oil
all-purpose flour
salt and pepper
4 Tbs. (½ stick) butter
3 lemons, halved

Dipped in seasoned flour before frying, the meat in this recipe is substantial enough to be served alone with just a simple salad or some sliced fresh tomatoes and basil. Very good. You can use the same method for pork tenderloin.

To make the scaloppine, put each cutlet between two pieces of plastic wrap and, using a mallet or rolling pin, gently flatten the meat until it is about ¼ inch thick.

Heat a large frying pan over high heat and add the vegetable oil. Season the flour with salt and pepper, and turn the scaloppine in this until evenly coated. Place the scaloppine in the pan and cook over high heat for 1 minute. Reduce the heat to medium and continue cooking until golden on the underside, about 2 minutes longer. Turn and cook for 1 minute or so on the other side.

Take the scaloppine from the pan and set aside. Leave the pan on the heat. Add the butter and season with some pepper. Let the butter melt and, as it starts to sizzle, squeeze in the juice of two of the lemon halves.

Put the scaloppine onto hot serving plates, add the sauce from the pan, and serve with a lemon half on each plate.

'BASIC RECIPE: BREADED VEAL SCALOPPINE'

¾ cup all-purpose flour

salt and pepper

2 eggs

a little milk

2 cups fine, dry bread crumbs

4 flattened veal scaloppine, about the size of your hand

vegetable oil for frying

What is important is that these little morsels are cooked fairly quickly, so that the meat cooks in the center to pink but the crumb coating stays beautifully golden and crisp.

Put the flour in a bowl and season well with salt and pepper. Beat the eggs and milk together in another bowl. Set these in a line with the flour first and the bread crumbs last in a third bowl.

Working with one scaloppine at a time, roll in the flour, then dip into the egg. Lift out and let the excess egg drain off, then coat in the bread crumbs. Pat firmly to make sure the scaloppine is thoroughly coated with crumbs.

Heat the oven to 300°F. Put a large, heavy frying pan on the stovetop and get it hot. Add 2 tablespoons of oil and, once the oil is hot, drop in two scaloppine. They should sizzle a little. Cook for about 4 minutes on each side until they are golden—not dark brown (lower or increase the heat to get the desired effect).

Put the cooked scaloppine in the oven to keep warm and repeat the process with the remaining scaloppine, adding more oil only if necessary. Serve with the fava bean and Romano mash (recipe on page 194), or one of the ideas on the following pages.

Tomato Sauce & Gruyère Cheese

Arugula, Parmesan & Capers

Chopped Hard-Cooked Eggs
with Anchovies & Parsley

Garlic Butter

Crisp Fried Potatoes & Mayonnaise

Lemon & Parsley Butter

Tartare sauce

Fried Egg & Anchovies

Tomato Sauce & Gruyère Cheese

For the best result, use good-quality canned Italian plum tomatoes.

4 Tbs. olive oil
1 onion, diced
1 garlic clove, crushed
1 tsp. flaked sea salt
1 tsp. ground black pepper
28-oz. can crushed tomatoes
8 slices Gruyère cheese

In a heavy saucepan, heat the oil over medium heat. Add the onion and cook for 3 minutes, stirring constantly. Add the garlic, salt, and pepper and cook for 2 minutes longer. Stir in the tomatoes and bring to a boil, then simmer for about 20 minutes, stirring occasionally.

   Heat the broiler. Top each breaded scaloppine with a big spoonful of sauce, then cover with a slice of Gruyère. Broil until just melted, or longer until bubbling and crisp. Serves 4 with some sauce left over for something else.

Arugula, Parmesan & Capers

Fresh, salty, and quick, this is a great way to eat breaded scaloppine. The salad has a kick from the peppery arugula and sharp, vinegary capers.

7 oz. arugula
about 4 oz. Parmesan cheese, grated or shaved
2 heaped Tbs. capers in brine
3 Tbs. olive oil
lemon wedges

Mix the arugula, cheese, capers, and oil together in a bowl, adding a teaspoon of the brine from the caper jar, too. Toss well and serve with the breaded scaloppine and lemon. Serves 4.

Chopped Hard-Cooked Eggs with Anchovies & Parsley

4 medium slices stale bread, with crusts, diced
1 tsp. salt
2 thick bacon slices, chopped
6 canned anchovies
1 garlic clove, crushed
1 fresh chile, chopped
2 hard-cooked eggs, chopped
large handful of chopped fresh parsley

Put the diced bread in a bowl and add the salt. Sprinkle with water, then toss the bread cubes until they are uniformly damp, but not soaked. Cover tightly and let stand for 1 hour.

   In a frying pan, fry the bacon and anchovies until browned, then remove them from the pan. Add the garlic, chile, and bread to the fat and fry, turning with a spatula, until the bread cubes are lightly toasted.

   Stir in the chopped eggs, parsley, bacon, and anchovies. Serve with the scaloppine. Serves 4.

Garlic Butter

Just saying "garlic butter" takes me back to when I was 17 and my first job—the first thing I did each day was prepare the garlic bread. This recipe makes a lot, which I think is well worth doing. The butter will keep in the refrigerator for a week or so.

3 garlic cloves, smashed and peeled
salt
2 tsp. Worcestershire sauce
⅔ cup salted butter
handful of minced fresh parsley

Sprinkle the garlic with some salt and crush to a paste using the flat side of a large knife. Mix with the Worcestershire sauce.

   Use an electric mixer to beat the butter until it turns white and fluffy, scraping down the sides of the bowl frequently. Add the garlic mixture and parsley and beat well.

   Shape the mixture into quenelles to serve on top of your veal. Wrap the rest up like a sausage in plastic wrap and store in the refrigerator.

Crisp Fried Potatoes & Mayonnaise

2 Tbs. olive oil
1 lb. fingerling or other small boiling potatoes,
  scrubbed and halved
2 Tbs. butter
2 tsp. capers
juice of ½ lemon
roughly chopped fresh tarragon
salt and pepper
mayonnaise
lemon wedges

Heat the oil in a large, heavy skillet. Add the potatoes and sauté until golden, then continue cooking for about 10 minutes, stirring all the time. The potatoes will caramelize and taste sweet.

  Add the butter and capers and fry until the capers start to pop and become crisp, 1–2 minutes. Add the lemon juice, tarragon, and seasoning. Serve the potatoes with the scaloppine, plus some mayonnaise and fresh lemon wedges. Serves 4.

Lemon & Parsley Butter

Lemon and parsley butter is not greasy, but is fresh, vibrant, and light. Being a bit sharp, it makes one of the very best things to serve with breaded scaloppine.

14 Tbs. (1¾ sticks) butter, cut into small cubes
salt
splash of white wine
juice of 1 large lemon
large handful of chopped fresh parsley
lemon wedges

Heat a frying pan until really hot, then add the butter and a sprinkle of salt. Pour in the wine as the butter starts to melt—it should melt fast and sizzle. If not, your pan isn't hot enough.

  Once the butter starts to bubble, add the lemon juice and bring to a boil. Stir in the parsley, then pour the sauce over the veal and serve with lemon wedges. Serves 4.

Hollandaise sauce

You don't have to refer to the recipe on page 130 because we've got it for you right here!

6 Tbs. white wine
6 Tbs. white-wine vinegar
20 black peppercorns
2 bay leaves
3 egg yolks
1¼ cups (2½ sticks) butter, melted and kept warm
pinch of salt
juice of ½ lemon

Boil the first four ingredients in a saucepan until reduced to 3 tablespoons, 5–8 minutes. Let cool, then strain.

  Put the yolks in a large stainless steel bowl set over a pan of steaming water. Whisk in a tablespoon of the vinegar mixture. Keep whisking until the mixture turns pale and the whisk leaves a pattern in it. Remove the bowl from the heat and gradually whisk in the butter. Add a tablespoon of water if you feel the sauce might be about to scramble. Add the salt and lemon juice. Serves 4.

Fried Egg & Anchovies

This great veal dish is named Holstein after the dairy cow that is the main source of veal. I love my fried eggs with crisp edges and the way to make that happen is as follows.

some oil, preferably olive
4 eggs
8 canned anchovies

Heat the oil in a large nonstick frying pan until quite hot. Drop your eggs in and let them start to spit and splutter—that is all part of the plan.

  Next, reduce the heat to low and cook until the white sets—at the last minute turn the heat up to full and cook for 30 seconds.

  Place a fried egg on each breaded scaloppine and lay a couple of anchovies on top. There you have it. Serves 4.

'BREADED VEAL WITH SPAGHETTI & TOMATO SAUCE'

7 oz. spaghetti

salt and pepper

3 Tbs. olive oil, plus extra
   for the pasta

8 oz. cherry tomatoes

1 garlic clove, chopped

handful of chopped fresh
   parsley

1 oz. Parmesan cheese shavings

Spaghetti is a classic Italian accompaniment to breaded veal scaloppine, and when you try it you will see why they like it this way.

Fill a pot with 2 quarts of water and set over high heat. Cook the pasta with some salt and a little oil, according to the directions on the package.

In another pan, heat the olive oil with the cherry tomatoes, using the back of a spoon to squash the tomatoes so they pop. Cook for 2 minutes, then add the garlic and season with salt and pepper.

Drain the pasta and add it to the tomato sauce. Stir it through, then throw in the parsley and stir again. Sprinkle with the Parmesan shavings, finish with black pepper, and serve hot alongside your scaloppine.

ALSO GOOD WITH SCALOPPINE: Wild mushrooms, parsley, and shallots ☛ Stuffed with ham and cheese ☛ Cream and mushroom sauce

'TOMATO, OLIVE & LEMON SALAD'

4 large plum (Roma) tomatoes
2/3 cup small purple or black
    olives
large handful of fresh flat-leaf
    parsley
2 small shallots, thinly sliced
flaked sea salt and pepper
1 lemon
3 Tbs. good-quality extra-virgin
    olive oil

Cut the tomatoes into small chunks. Put the olives on a board and, using the palm of your hand, push down to squash each olive, then remove the pit. Roughly chop the parsley on the same board, so it takes up the olive juice.

Put the tomatoes in a mixing bowl with the shallots. Give them a generous grind of pepper and a sprinkle of sea salt. Finely grate the rind from the lemon and add to the bowl, then squeeze the juice and add it, too. Stir well and leave for 10 minutes. Add the olives, parsley, and olive oil, and serve.

'VEAL SALTIMBOCCA'

8 slices prosciutto
8 small veal scaloppine, about
    the size of your palm
pepper
8 fresh sage leaves
3 Tbs. olive oil
7 Tbs. butter
juice of 1 large lemon, plus
    4 lemon wedges for serving

Translated literally as "jump in the mouth," saltimbocca is traditionally served alone.

Lay two slices of prosciutto flat on a clean surface and place a scaloppine in the center of each slice. Season the meat with pepper only as the ham is salty. Stick a sage leaf on top of each scaloppine, then carefully fold the prosciutto over the veal so it starts to wrap it but not tightly. Repeat until all the scaloppine are wrapped up. Refrigerate for about 10 minutes to set.

Heat the oven to 300°F. Set a heavy-based frying pan over high heat. If it is not large enough to cook all the saltimbocca at one time, work in batches. Pour a little oil into the hot pan and carefully add the veal. Sear for 2 minutes on each side, then remove and keep warm in the oven while you sear the others.

Once all the saltimbocca are in the oven, drop the butter into the frying pan. When it's half melted, squeeze in the lemon juice. Drizzle this sauce over the saltimbocca and serve two per person with a wedge of lemon.

'VEAL SCALOPPINE WITH EGG & PARMESAN'

2 eggs

4 canned anchovies, finely
   chopped

1¾ cups freshly grated
   Parmesan cheese

½ handful of chopped fresh
   flat-leaf parsley

pepper

1 cup arugula

¼ cup olive oil

¼ cup vegetable oil

4 veal scaloppine, about
   4 oz. each

all-purpose flour

4 Tbs. (½ stick) butter

2 tsp. white-wine vinegar

1 lemon, quartered

I love this and cannot eat enough of it. Dipped in a light frying batter, the veal is substantial enough to be served alone, with just a little arugula salad alongside.

Whisk the eggs together for 1 minute until light. Stir in the anchovies, Parmesan, parsley, and ½ teaspoon freshly ground black pepper.

Place the arugula in the bottom of four shallow serving dishes and dress with the olive oil and some black pepper.

To cook the veal, set two large frying pans over high heat and add the vegetable oil. Turn the scaloppine in the flour until evenly coated, and then dip in the cheesy egg mixture.

Place two scaloppine in each of the pans and cook for 1 minute. Reduce the heat to medium and cook until golden on the underside, about 2 minutes longer. Turn and cook on the other side for 2–3 minutes.

Add half of the butter to each frying pan. When it has melted, pour half of the vinegar into each, tilting the pans to combine the juices.

Lift out the scaloppine and lay them on the arugula. Drizzle the buttery pan juices over the veal and serve with lemon wedges.

'VITELLO TONNATO'

1 egg yolk

2 tsp. white vinegar

1 tsp. Dijon mustard

1 small can tuna in oil, drained,
   or 4 oz. leftover cooked tuna

7 Tbs. good-quality olive oil

salt and pepper

1 lemon, cut into 6 wedges

1-lb. piece cold, boneless
   roast veal

chopped fresh chives for garnish

1 loaf bread

I love the Italians. Only they would be brave enough to invent a dish using leftover roast veal and leftover tuna. But you have to hand it to them, because it really works. Soft meat and salty tuna mayonnaise makes a very clever combination.

Drop the egg yolk into a bowl, add the vinegar, and whisk until white. Add the mustard and tuna, then drizzle in all but about 1 tablespoon of the oil and beat to make a mayonnaise. Taste and season with salt and pepper, then squeeze in the juice of two lemon wedges.

Slice the meat as thinly as possible and lay it out on four serving plates, or one big platter. Sprinkle with the remaining olive oil and some chives, then pour the dressing over the meat in a squiggly pattern, like a child making a mess. Add the lemon wedges and serve with the bread.

'OSSO BUCO'

4 large osso buco (crosscut
   veal shank)
salt and pepper
handful of all-purpose flour
⅓ cup oil
2 carrots, peeled
1 onion, peeled
2 celery ribs
2 garlic cloves
2 bay leaves
4 cups beef stock (recipe on
   page 22), or other light stock

gremolata
handful of fresh flat-leaf parsley
1 garlic clove
1 lemon

Osso buco is a great Italian dish of braised veal shank. The name translates as "bone" and "hole."

Heat the oven to 400°F. Season the veal pieces really well with salt and pepper. Coat them in the flour, then grind a bit more pepper over them.

Heat a large, heavy frying pan. Add the oil and the meat at the same time and let the veal start to brown. When golden, after about 2 minutes, turn it over and cook on the other side for 2 minutes. Meanwhile, put all the vegetables and garlic in a food processor and mince them (or mince with a knife).

Take the meat out of the pan and lay it in a casserole or baking dish. Add the minced vegetables and herbs to the frying pan and cook, stirring, until the mixture is soft and smells like vegetable soup, about 5 minutes. Place the cooked vegetables over the meat and pour the stock over the top. Cover with the lid or a sheet of foil and braise in the oven for 2 hours.

While the osso buco is cooking, make the gremolata. Using a sharp knife, mince the parsley, then mince the garlic. Take a fine grater and remove the rind from the lemon. Combine the parsley, garlic, and lemon rind in a small bowl and season with some salt and pepper. Stir well and set aside (gremolata doesn't keep well, so try to use it the day it is made).

Take the osso buco from the oven. I like it soupy, but if you want a thicker sauce pour the pan juices into a saucepan and boil them until they have reduced to a thick sauce. Sprinkle the gremolata over the osso buco and serve with mashed potatoes or rice.

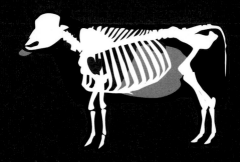

OFFAL

There are many parts of the world where offal (also called variety meats or organ meats) is considered the finest of all cuts of any animal. In Thailand, old recipes for offal would have been written for the royal palace, as all offal was reserved for the royal family. We in the West have a varied attitude to offal—some people are scared of it and some love it. Like politics and religion, it will divide a dinner table more quickly than the announcement that someone's partner is having an affair. But I do urge you to try it. Good offal is delicious and rich in flavor. Each cut requires a different cooking method. The recipes here are tasty, reliable, and not over-the-top—I have tried to give you a gentle introduction to the subject. The sweetbreads in particular are fantabuloso.

'BASIC RECIPE: SWEETBREADS'

2–3 large sweetbreads (heart sweetbreads)
1 carrot
1 celery rib
1 shallot
2 bay leaves
parsley stems (optional)
black peppercorns
splash of white wine
2 caps white vinegar
salt and pepper

It's funny that some people think sweetbreads are testicles—members of my family still do, no matter how many times I tell them that sweetbreads don't come from anywhere near that part of an animal's body. Sweetbreads are one of two things: they are either the gland that surrounds the heart (these are about the size of your hand and really expensive), or they are thyroid glands from the throat, and are much smaller. This recipe is for the large heart sweetbreads. If you have small sweetbreads, simply simmer them for a shorter period.

Soak the sweetbreads in a bowl of cold water for 20 minutes, then drain. Use a very sharp knife to take the membrane off, plus any excess fat. Put the vegetables, herbs, peppercorns, wine, and vinegar in a big saucepan with 4 cups water and bring it slowly to a boil. Once it comes to a boil, sprinkle in some salt and some pepper, then simmer gently for 10 minutes (or less if you are using small sweetbreads). Take the pan off the heat.

Now you have options. You can let the sweetbreads cool in the cooking liquid, then slice and shallow fry them. Alternatively, you can bake them whole, or wrapped in something. For this, take them out of the cooking liquid while still hot and put them on a wire rack. Roll them in plastic wrap so you have a tight cylinder; tie at both ends and prick with a pin. Once they are cold, unwrap and cook according to the recipe.

'FRIED SWEETBREADS, PEAS AND PANCETTA'

2 large cooked sweetbreads
   (recipe on page 215), cooled in
   the cooking liquid, then
   drained
about 3 Tbs. vegetable oil
3 shallots, diced
1 garlic clove, minced
salt and pepper
4 oz. finely sliced pancetta, cut
   into strips
10 oz. boiled new potatoes
1⅓ cups frozen green peas
12 artichoke hearts packed
   in oil, sliced
4 Tbs. (½ stick) butter

Cut the prepared sweetbreads the same thickness as your thumb. Heat the oil slowly in a large frying pan and add the shallots and garlic. Cook for a few minutes, then take them out of the pan and set aside. Drop the sweetbreads into the pan, adding some more oil if needed, and let them cook for about 2 minutes on each side —they must be crisp. Season the sweetbreads with salt and pepper on both sides as they cook.

Take the sweetbreads out of the pan and set aside. Add the pancetta and potatoes to the pan and fry until lightly browned. Put the cooked shallots and garlic back in the pan, then add the frozen peas, artichokes, and butter. When everything is hot, season with some salt and pepper.

Remove the pan from the heat. Add the crisp-fried sweetbreads and toss. Taste and season again if necessary, then serve.

'SWEETBREADS WITH SAUCE POIVRADE'

4 slices brioche

2 large cooked sweetbreads
(recipe on page 215), cooled in
the cooking liquid, then
drained

1½ Tbs. butter

1½ Tbs. olive oil

sauce

7 Tbs. butter

3 cups finely diced carrots

1½ cups finely diced celery

1 cup finely diced shallots

1½ cups black peppercorns,
ground and then sifted

⅔ cup red-currant jelly

1¼ cups malt vinegar

½ cup gravy (recipes on pages
33 and 153)

This pepper sauce is both sweet and hot, but also sticky. It works well hot or cold. You'll probably have lots left over, but you can also serve it with game birds and turkey—it's far better than cranberry sauce. It is important that you sift the freshly ground peppercorns before adding them to the sauce.

Start with the sauce. Melt the butter in a saucepan. Add the vegetables and sweat until tender. Stir in the pepper and cook for 10 minutes longer. Add the red-currant jelly and malt vinegar, bring to a boil, and reduce until sticky. Add the gravy. When boiling again, remove from the heat. Taste and season.

Toast the brioche; keep warm while you cook the sweetbreads. Cut the sweetbreads the same thickness as your thumb. Combine the butter and olive oil in a hot frying pan. Add the sweetbreads (without seasoning them) and fry until colored on each side. Deglaze the pan with about ⅓ cup of sauce poivrade and bring it to a boil, then serve on the toasted brioche.

'SWEETBREADS IN PANCETTA WITH CHAMP & BLACK CABBAGE'

12 slices pancetta, or prosciutto
2 large cooked sweetbreads
(recipe on page 215), cooled,
wrapped in plastic
salt and pepper
1 Tbs. olive oil
2 lemons, halved

champ

2½ lb. potatoes, peeled
6 Tbs. unsalted butter
6 scallions
2–3 Tbs. heavy cream

black cabbage

6 leaves cavolo nero (Tuscan
black cabbage)
4 large shallots, minced
1 garlic clove, crushed
3 Tbs. butter
splash of vegetable oil
chicken stock
bunch of fresh thyme, leaves
picked from stems

By wrapping sweetbreads in pancetta, the bacon both protects the meat and adds saltiness. I prefer pancetta to prosciutto, because it is smokier and, being so thin and streaked with lard, it looks very attractive, but the choice is up to you.

Start with the champ. Put the potatoes in a large saucepan with enough cold salted water to cover. Bring to a boil and simmer until just tender, about 20 minutes. When ready, drain.

Meanwhile, trim the cavolo nero leaves and wash them well. In a large saucepan, sweat the shallots and garlic in the butter and oil until soft but not colored. Add the cavolo nero and just enough chicken stock to cover. Bring to a boil and add the thyme. Cook uncovered until the cabbage is tender, about 15 minutes. Season with pepper—it shouldn't need much salt. Keep warm until ready to serve.

Heat the oven to 400°F. On a large piece of foil, arrange six slices of pancetta (or prosciutto) so that they overlap each other slightly. Season one sweetbread with black pepper—no salt, because the bacon adds the salt—and put it into the center of the pancetta. Use the foil to help you roll the sweetbread in the pancetta, making sure it is completely enclosed. Twist the ends of the foil package like a sausage. Repeat with the remaining pancetta and sweetbread.

Heat the oil in a heavy-based stovetop-to-oven casserole. Put the foil packages in the pan and cook for 2 minutes or so, then turn them over and cook for about 5 minutes longer. Transfer to the oven and bake for just under 10 minutes. Remove the casserole from the oven and let the sweetbreads rest for at least 5 minutes.

Mash the potatoes well with a fork or potato masher. Mix in two-thirds of the butter and season to taste with salt and pepper. Roughly chop the scallions, keeping the green and white parts separate.

Bring the cream and remaining butter to a boil in a medium-sized saucepan. Stir in the white parts of the scallions and the mashed potatoes and stir vigorously over medium heat for 4–5 minutes.

Remove the pan from the heat. Mix in the green parts of the scallions and season to taste. Cover and keep warm.

With a sharp knife, carve the sweetbreads into slices, cutting through the foil. Discard the foil and serve the sweetbreads with the champ, lemon halves, and a bowl of black cabbage on the side. The pancetta will be just cooked and the sweetbreads slightly pink.

Variation If you want to make plain mashed potatoes, follow the instructions for champ, leaving out the scallions.

'SWEETBREAD WELLINGTONS'

2 sheets puff pastry (preferably
    made with butter), about 10 oz.
4 oz. pâté
2 large, cooked sweetbreads
    (recipe on page 215), cooled
    wrapped in plastic
1 egg, beaten
mustard sauce (recipe on
    page 131)

Sweetbread Wellingtons is a real luxury dish. I love anything wrapped in pastry and this is no exception.

Lay the pastry sheets on the work surface and spread the pâté over them. Place the sweetbreads on top and brush all around the edges with beaten egg. Wrap the sweetbreads in the pastry, then turn them over so the seams are on the bottom. Prick the pastry packages on top twice to let out the steam during baking, then brush them all over with lots of beaten egg. Put them on a baking sheet in the freezer for 10 minutes.

Heat the oven to 400°F. Bake the Wellingtons for 40 minutes. Slice and serve them with the mustard sauce.

'TONGUE'

1 beef tongue
½ head celery root, peeled
   and chopped
1 onion, peeled and halved
2 fresh thyme sprigs
2 bay leaves
6 black peppercorns
pinch of salt

Soak the tongue in a bowl of cold water for 30 minutes to remove all the blood. Drain and place in a pot. Add enough fresh water to cover and bring to a boil, then drain and refresh under cold running water. Drain well.

Put the tongue back in the pot, cover again with water, and add the vegetables, herbs, peppercorns, and salt. Cut out a disk of parchment paper the same diameter as the pan, cut a hole in the center, and press it down onto the surface of the liquid, to keep the tongue submerged. Bring to a boil, then simmer gently for 1 hour and 40 minutes. Let the tongue cool in the liquid.

Once cool, peel the tongue by sliding a knife under the skin; if properly cooked it will pull off easily.

'FRENCH DRESSED TONGUE'

7 oz. cooked beef tongue (recipe
   above)
4 handfuls of mâche

dressing
1 tsp. Dijon mustard
1 Tbs. champagne vinegar
2 Tbs. olive oil
3 Tbs. vegetable oil
2 tsp. hot water
salt and pepper

Put the mustard in a small mixing bowl. Whisk in the vinegar slowly, followed by both oils, still whisking slowly to emulsify the dressing. Thin with the hot water and season to taste.

Finely slice the tongue and arrange it on four serving plates. Spoon some of the dressing over the tongue and top each plate with a handful of mâche.

'SAUCE GRIBICHE'

4 hard-cooked eggs
2 hard-cooked egg yolks
½ Tbs. Dijon mustard
salt and pepper
½ Tbs. white-wine vinegar
1 cup olive oil
bunch of fresh chervil, chopped
½ bunch of fresh tarragon,
   chopped
¼ cup capers, drained and
   chopped
½ cup cornichons (tiny, tart
   pickled gherkins), drained
   and chopped

A great sauce to serve with tongue, this is essentially a mayonnaise, but the egg yolks are cooked instead of raw. I like to make a lot and then keep it in the refrigerator to eat with cold ham, too. It's also good as a salad dressing.

Put the whole eggs and yolks, mustard, and some salt and pepper in a large bowl and mash them well together. To this paste add the vinegar and then the olive oil, drop by drop as if making mayonnaise. Keep the sauce creamy by adding small amounts of vinegar or warm water, as necessary.

Finish the sauce by adding the chopped herbs, capers, and cornichons. Taste and correct the seasoning.

To serve, arrange slices of tongue on plates and drop the sauce on top in small dollops.

'VEAL KIDNEYS WITH SPINACH & MADEIRA'

2 Tbs. butter
4 oz. spinach leaves
8 oz. veal kidneys
vegetable oil
salt and pepper

madeira jus
1 cup madeira
½ cup port
½ cup beef stock (recipe on
    page 22)

First make the madeira sauce. Put the madeira, port, and stock in a saucepan and bring to a boil. Boil hard until the volume has reduced to ⅔ cup. That's it! Keep warm until ready to serve.

Heat the butter in a large saucepan, add the spinach, and cook, stirring, until the spinach has wilted. Keep hot.

Heat a ridged cast-iron grill pan or broiler pan until hot. Cut the kidneys into slices the width of your finger. Rub with oil and add a bit of seasoning, then pan-grill the kidney slices for no more than 2 minutes on each side.

Arrange the hot buttered spinach on serving plates. Lay the kidneys on top and spoon the sauce around.

'ROASTED VEAL KIDNEY WITH MUSHROOM SAUCE'

1 whole veal kidney in its
  own fat
salt and pepper
2 tsp. paprika
1 fresh rosemary sprig

mushroom sauce
7 oz. mixed wild mushrooms
2 tsp. olive oil
2 tsp. butter
1 large shallot, diced
2 Tbs. crème fraîche

Veal kidneys are naturally encased in suet, which is usually trimmed off, but for this recipe you want the suet left on so you can slowly roast the kidney in its own fat. If you can't get a kidney with the fat still on it, just spread it with lots of butter.

Heat the oven to 400°F. Rub the kidney all over with salt, pepper, and paprika. Lay the rosemary in a small roasting pan and set the kidney on top. Roast for 50–60 minutes, basting after 20 minutes and then again at 40 minutes.

Clean the mushrooms by wiping them with a damp cloth. Place a large, heavy pan over high heat. Add the oil and butter and then the shallot. Cook for 3 minutes until it starts to color. Add the mushrooms and season well with pepper and salt. Cook for 4 minutes. Turn the mushrooms over and cook for 2 minutes longer. Mix in the crème fraîche and take the pan from the heat. Serve with the kidney.

'TRIPE ROMAN STYLE'

4½ lb. honeycomb tripe, prepared by the butcher

2 bay leaves

salt and pepper

1½ cups olive oil

2½ cups diced carrots

1½ cups diced onions

1 cup chopped garlic

1 cup white wine

2 cups diced fresh tomatoes

2 cups gravy (recipe on pages 33 and 153)

2 cups freshly grated Parmesan cheese

2 cups grated Romano cheese

2 cups fresh mint leaves, chopped

Put the tripe in a pot with the bay leaves and cover generously with salted water. Simmer slowly until the tripe is soft, about 3 hours. Take the tripe from the cooking liquid and let it cool before cutting it into strips the size of your little finger. Strain the broth and keep 1 cup for the sauce.

Heat the olive oil in a deep, heavy-based saucepan and sauté the carrots, onions, and garlic until well browned. Add the white wine and let it bubble until it has reduced to a glaze. Add the tomatoes and cook for 5 minutes longer.

Add the tripe, tomato, gravy, and the reserved cooking liquid. Bring to a boil and let boil until the liquid has reduced by two-thirds in volume. Taste and adjust the seasoning, then let the tripe cool.

Before serving, heat the tripe and boil it fast so the sauce starts to reduce and fry. Add the cheeses and cook, stirring, until the tripe is coated with the sauce and the sauce is very sticky. Add the chopped mint and serve.

'PAN-GRILLED CALF'S LIVER WITH SHERRY, BACON, & SCALLION MASH'

bunch of scallions
½ cup heavy cream
3 cups mashed potatoes
  (recipe on page 219)
salt and pepper
12 slices bacon
olive oil
4 slices calf's liver, about
  5 oz. each
½ cup sherry
4 small bouquets of watercress
  (optional)

Liver and mashed potatoes are great together, but this sherry sauce, which is not sweet but lovely and sharp, makes this dish very special indeed.

Preheat the broiler. Wash the scallions and discard the outer layer, then cut them into rounds, keeping the green and white parts separate.

In a stainless steel saucepan, bring the cream to a boil with the white parts of the scallion and cook for 1 minute. Stir in the mashed potatoes and adjust the seasoning, mixing thoroughly. Make sure the mash bubbles. Keep hot.

Meanwhile, broil the bacon until crisp, and keep hot.

Heat a ridged cast-iron grill pan or broiler pan over high heat. Season the liver well with salt and pepper and pour on a liberal amount of olive oil. When the grill pan is hot, drop the liver onto it and cook over high heat for 3 minutes on each side. Pour in the sherry and remove from the heat—the sherry will continue to bubble and make the delicious sauce.

Mix the green parts of the scallions with the mashed potatoes and spoon some in the center of each serving plate. Place the liver on top, pour the sauce from the pan over this, and top with the bacon. Garnish with watercress, if desired.

'STUFFED BEEF HEART'

1 large beef heart, trimmed, boned, and split lengthwise

salt and pepper

¼ cup vegetable oil, plus extra for the heart

2 heaped cups bread stuffing mix, prepared according to the package directions

2 carrots, chopped

5 fresh sage leaves

½ cup beef stock (recipe on page 22)

2 Tbs. red wine

1 tsp. cornstarch

In Australia, there is a dish called colonial goose, which is a lamb shoulder stuffed and served with the leg end up to look like a goose. We also have mock goose, which is stuffed heart. Here is a quick recipe for making it using bought dried stuffing. It works just as well for lamb hearts; just don't cook them as long.

Wash the heart and remove the arteries if your butcher hasn't done this already. Soak it in cold water with 2 teaspoons salt for half an hour. Drain and dry the heart, then rub inside and out with oil and season with lots of pepper and salt.

Heat the oven to 275°F. Fill the heart with the stuffing and close the end with a skewer. Heat the oil in a Dutch oven and fry the heart to give it color. Take it out and set aside. Drop the carrots into the pot, then add the sage and stock. Return the heart to the pot. Cover and place in the oven to cook for 6 hours.

Take the heart out of the casserole and set aside. To make a sauce from the pan juices, mix the red wine into the cornstarch, add the mixture to the juices, and stir over medium-high heat until the sauce comes to a boil and thickens. Remove immediately from the heat and serve the sauce with the heart.

Tip You could simply thicken the sauce with some instant gravy instead of using the mix of cornstarch and wine.

'SAVORY MEATBALLS'

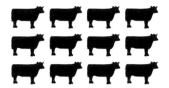

8 oz. ground pork (about 1 cup)

8 oz. veal kidneys

8 oz. calf's liver

1½ oz. bacon

1½ oz. pork fatback

3 oz. foie gras (optional)

½ cup white bread crumbs

salt and pepper

2 Tbs. butter

2 onions, diced

5 garlic cloves, crushed

1 egg

scant 1 cup fresh sage leaves, chopped

½ cup fresh tarragon, chopped

caul fat

handful of diced carrots

handful of diced leek

handful of diced celery

2 cups beef stock (recipe on page 22)

I was a non-offal man when I lived in Australia. Since moving to the UK, I have learned that the secret is plenty (and I do mean plenty) of seasoning. These tasty meatballs, which the British—traditionally but rather unfortunately—call faggots, need lots of black pepper and salt, as well as some herbs if you wish.

Ask your butcher if he will grind all the meat together, or do it yourself, in batches, using a meat grinder or food processor. Grind each type of meat separately. Once it is all ground, put it in a large mixing bowl and mix well, beating it for a few minutes. Add the bread crumbs and season with lots of salt and pepper.

Heat a frying pan over medium heat. Add the butter, then add about three-quarters of the onions and cook until soft but not colored, 4–5 minutes. Add the garlic and cook for 2–3 minutes. Set aside to cool.

Stir the egg, sage, and tarragon into the onions and garlic, then mix with the ground meat. Refrigerate to chill.

Heat the oven to 425°F. Rinse the caul fat, then soak it in a bowl of cold water for 10 minutes. Drain thoroughly.

Lay the caul fat out on the worktop and cut it into 5-inch squares. Roll the meat mixture into balls the size of a tennis ball and wrap each one in a piece of caul fat. Sprinkle the remaining onion and the other diced vegetables over the bottom of a large roasting pan. Place the meatballs on top and season them. Pour in the stock, then cover the pan with foil and seal the edges well.

Put the pan in the oven, reduce the heat to 350°F, and cook for 30 minutes. Remove the foil, increase the temperature to 425°F and cook for 15 minutes longer. Serve with mashed potatoes and onion gravy (recipe on page 33).

'SCOTCH PIES'

meatball mixture (recipe on
  page 231)
butter for greasing

pastry
2 cups all-purpose flour
½ tsp. salt
⅓ cup beef drippings
¾ cup water

Scotch pies are normally made with lamb, but I like to use an offal mixture for savory meatballs. The pies must be peppery, so season well.

Make the pastry the day before baking: Sift the flour and salt into a bowl. Combine ¾ cup of water and the drippings in a saucepan and stir over medium heat until the drippings melt. Remove from the heat. Make a well in the center of the flour and add the liquid, stirring to make a dough. Wrap in plastic wrap and refrigerate overnight to rest.

The next day, heat the oven to 375°F and grease four 4-inch baking rings to hold the pies. Roll out the dough thinly and cut out four large rounds to be used as the shells and four smaller rounds for the top crusts. Put the rings on a baking sheet and use the large rounds to line them. Fill all the way to the top with the meatball mixture. Dampen the rims of the pastry shells with water, put the top crusts on, and press to seal. Cut a little hole in the top of each pie, then bake for 40 minutes.

You can eat the pies hot or cold.

SWEET

Gregg Wallace, with whom I present *Masterchef* on television in the UK, swears that the best desserts in the world are British, and I tend to agree. Britain's desserts are steeped in history, and in suet—yes, beef suet, the hard fat from around the animal's kidneys. The great plum pudding is not a Christmas dessert without suet—the flavor is just not right. The recipes I've given here are not going to win any awards for presentation, but they will satisfy you and keep you warm (which you need in a British climate). For Christmas, I like to give presents that I have made myself, and mincemeat, for making mince pies, is a very nice gift.

'CLASSIC MINCEMEAT'

Makes about 6½ lb.

2¼ lb. tart baking apples

3¾ cups packed dark
brown sugar

½ cup dark rum

1 lb. ground or finely chopped
beef suet

grated rind of 2 lemons

grated rind of 2 oranges

2 Tbs. apple-pie spice

2 tsp. ground cinnamon

2 tsp. grated nutmeg

1 lb. diced mixed candied
citrus peel (about 3 cups)

1 lb. raisins (about 3 cups)

1 lb. golden raisins (about
3 cups)

1 lb. currants (about 3 cups)

½ cup brandy

This is the basis of the best mince pie and is also brilliant for stuffed baked apples. Originally, meat was kept in molasses and other sugars to preserve it, but now the mixture is predominately dried fruit with some suet included to keep it moist when baked.

Heat the oven to 120°F. Peel and grate the apples, then mix with the sugar and rum in a Dutch oven. Stir in the suet. Cover, place in the oven, and cook for 4 hours, stirring every hour.

Put all the rest of the ingredients, except the brandy, in a very large bowl. Add the cooked apples and stir well. Let cool—the dried fruit will soak up the juices.

When it's all cool, add the brandy and stir again. Spoon the mincemeat into sterilized jars, seal, and keep in a dark, cool place (for long storage, process in a boiling-water bath). A jar of mincemeat makes a great Christmas present!

'MINCE PIES'

1 lb. refrigerated or homemade
   piecrust
2 cups mincemeat (recipe on
   page 237)
a little milk
2 Tbs. sugar

**The British like little mince pies—maybe because they
have more pastry than mincemeat—and there are
many versions of this recipe. I like lots of sugar
sprinkled on top as it makes the pies sweet and the
pastry crunchy. The pies are best eaten once they have
cooled, because then they will have a bit of juice in
the bottom.**

Heat the oven to 400°F. Roll out the pastry to about ½ inch thick.
Cut out disks slightly larger than individual tartlet pans or a
12-hole small muffin pan. Use to line the pans.

Fill each pastry shell almost to the top with mincemeat, leaving
a little room so the filling can swell a bit during baking. Cut out
disks from the remaining pastry for the top crusts and cover the
filling, pinching the edges together to seal.

Brush the top crusts with milk and sprinkle with sugar. Slash two
slits in the top to allow the steam to escape.

Set the tartlet pans, or muffin pan, on a rimmed baking sheet (in
case any juice leaks out) and bake the pies for 35 minutes. Let
cool a little before removing from the pans.

'PLUM PUDDING'

Makes 4 puddings

1 large white loaf
2 cups all-purpose flour
1 cup ground or finely chopped
  beef suet
1 Earl Grey teabag
1 cup boiling water
grated rind of 1 lemon
grated rind of 1 orange
2 cups diced mixed candied
  citrus peel
1⅓ cups mixed raisins, golden
  raisins, and currants
2 tart baking apples, peeled
  and grated
1½ cups chopped blanched
  almonds
½ cup brandy
4 cups packed dark brown sugar
2 Tbs. apple-pie spice
2 tsp. ground cinnamon
2 tsp. grated nutmeg
½ cup dark rum
6 eggs
2 cups dark beer
butter for greasing

You could halve this recipe, and make only two puddings, but it is nice to give friends a pudding as a Christmas gift. On Christmas Day, boil your pudding for 1 hour and serve with brandy butter or hard sauce.

Trim off and discard the crusts from the loaf of bread. Place the rest in a food processor and pulse to make crumbs. Mix with the flour and suet, and leave somewhere warm.

Make some tea using the teabag and boiling water, then discard the teabag and add the lemon and orange rind. Put all the dried fruit, grated apples, and almonds in a big bowl, pour the tea mixture over them, and leave overnight.

The next day, drain any excess liquid from the dried fruit mixture and pour in the brandy. Mix the brown sugar with the spices and rum. Beat in the eggs, then add the beer. Pour this mixture over the fruit. Add the bread-crumb mixture and mix together using your hands and arms, right up to your elbows.

Butter four 2-quart ceramic pudding basins, steamed-pudding molds, or other heatproof bowls and fill them with the pudding mixture. Cover with parchment paper and then with foil, tying it on with string so the water cannot get into the pudding. Put a folded dishtowel in the bottom of a large pot and set the basins on it. Add enough water to come three-quarters of the way up the sides of the basins. Boil the puddings for 3 hours, replenishing the water as necessary.

Take the puddings out of the pot and let cool, then remove the foil, leaving the paper on. Cover with fresh foil, tie on with string, and store in a cool place ready for Christmas.

'BAKED APPLES & CUSTARD SAUCE'

½ cup ground or finely chopped
   beef suet

¾ cup packed light brown sugar

2 cups grated baking apples

⅔ cup golden raisins

⅓ heaped cup raisins

½ cup chopped prunes

⅓ cup chopped walnuts

⅓ cup chopped almonds

1 tsp. ground cinnamon

½ tsp. apple-pie spice

1 generous shot dark rum

1 generous shot brandy

10 whole baking apples

⅔ cup butter

confectioners' sugar for sifting

vanilla custard sauce

1 quart milk

8 egg yolks

½ cup + 2 Tbs. vanilla-flavored
   sugar

⅓ cup cornstarch

¼ cup all-purpose flour

½ cup brandy

This makes a lot of custard sauce and you can halve the recipe if you prefer, although custard is also delicious cold or can be reheated the next day. I find that people love it so much they always want more.

Heat the oven to 400°F. In a mixing bowl combine the suet, sugar, grated apples, dried fruit, nuts, spices, rum, and brandy. Stir well and set aside.

Slice off a little of the top and the base of each baking apple (so that it will sit flat). Halfway down the sides of the apples, make an incision in the peel all the way around the middle (so that the apples don't explode as they cook). Remove the cores.

Stuff each apple with as much of the dried fruit mixture as you can get in—there is plenty, so be generous and let some spill out over the top. Put the stuffed apples in a large roasting pan and top each one with some of the butter, pushing it in with your finger so the butter is inside. Sift some confectioners' sugar over the top. Bake for 20 minutes.

Meanwhile, make the custard: Heat the milk in a saucepan until scalding, then take the pan off the heat immediately. In a large bowl, beat together the egg yolks, vanilla sugar, cornstarch, and flour. Pour the hot milk slowly into the egg mixture, beating well.

Return the custard to the saucepan and cook over low heat, stirring, for a few minutes until the mixture thickens. Stir in the brandy. Remove from the heat and set aside in a warm place.

Take the apples from the oven. Carefully drain off the pan juices and serve them as a sauce with the apples and custard sauce.

'STEAMED MARMALADE PUDDING WITH BLOOD ORANGES'

⅓ cup butter, plus extra for greasing

granulated sugar for dusting

⅓ cup orange marmalade

1½ cups packed dark brown sugar

1½ Tbs. molasses

2 eggs

½ tsp. baking powder

2 tsp. ground ginger

2⅓ cups self-rising flour, sifted

⅓ cup ground or finely chopped beef suet

4 blood oranges

vanilla custard sauce (recipe on page 240)

Cleverly disguised as an elegant, grown-up dessert, these individual puddings topped with marmalade are sticky and sweet. They really are comfort food at its very best. The hot pudding combined with the slightly bitter orange and sweet custard is a real taste treat.

Heat the oven to 400°F. Grease eight small, individual, steamed-pudding molds or ramekins with a little butter and sprinkle with granulated sugar. Spoon a generous quantity of marmalade into the bottom of each mold and set aside.

In a mixing bowl, cream together the butter, brown sugar, and molasses. Stir in the eggs one at a time, then add the baking powder and ground ginger.

In a separate bowl, rub the flour and suet together. Add to the butter and egg mixture and stir well.

Spoon the batter into the molds—they should be three-quarters full. Put a dishtowel in the bottom of a roasting pan (if using metal molds for the puddings, this will prevent them from becoming too hot). Set the molds on top and pour enough hot water into the pan to come halfway up the sides of the molds.

Bake the puddings until firm to the touch, about 40 minutes. Remove from the oven and let settle for 10–15 minutes. (The puddings can be baked in advance, then reheated later in a 325°F oven for about 8 minutes; or unmolded, covered with plastic wrap, and heated in a microwave on HIGH for 90 seconds.)

Peel and slice the blood oranges, then spread them out on serving plates. Gently press around the edges of the puddings with your fingertips, to pull the sides away from the molds, and unmold onto the blood oranges. Serve with the custard sauce.

'GOLDEN SYRUP DUMPLINGS'

2 cups self-rising flour
½ cup ground or finely chopped
    beef suet
3 Tbs. sugar
1¼ cups golden syrup
vanilla custard sauce (recipe on
    page 240) or cream for serving

Golden syrup is a British staple—rich and golden, with a unique flavor. You could use light corn syrup, if you can't find golden syrup in your supermarket or gourmet market. These sweet versions of the suet dumpling are cooked in golden syrup and water, and the cooking liquid is then reduced to make a sauce.

Mix the flour, suet, and sugar together in a large bowl. Stir in about ½ cup warm water, or enough to make a heavy dough.

In a wide saucepan, sauté pan, or wok, combine the golden syrup and 4 cups of water and bring to a boil. Roll the dough into balls about the size of a golf ball.

Cooking in batches of 12 at a time, drop the dumplings into the boiling syrup. After about 5 minutes they will float to the top, which means they are cooked. At this point roll them over and let cook for another minute or so, then remove from the syrup and set aside while you cook the remaining dumplings.

When the dumplings are all cooked, fast-boil the cooking liquid to reduce it to about 2 cups. Drop all the dumplings into this sauce and toss them so they are well coated. Serve hot, with custard sauce or cream.

Variation Leave out the jam and add ⅔ cup golden raisins to the dough. Shape it into a log and steam. The British call this spotted dick.

'JAM ROLY POLY'

1³/₄ tsp. baking powder

1½ cups all-purpose flour

½ cup ground or finely chopped beef suet

¼ cup warm milk

grated rind and juice of 1 lemon

2 eggs

1⅓ cups chunky jam

vanilla custard sauce (recipe on page 240), cream, or ice cream for serving

If you are going to steam the pudding in the oven, heat it to 400°F. Mix the baking powder and flour together in a bowl and rub in the suet to give a mixture the texture of bread crumbs.

Combine the warm milk with the lemon rind and juice (be sure the milk is warm—if too hot, it will curdle). Beat in the eggs. Pour into the flour mixture and stir to form a dough.

Roll out the dough to a square about ³/₄ inch thick. Cover it with parchment paper and then with a large sheet of foil. Flip the whole thing over so the dough is on top. Spread the jam over evenly. Roll up the dough into a big sausage shape, wrap in the paper and foil, and twist the ends to secure them.

Set in a water-filled roasting pan to steam in the oven, or on a rack in a pan of gently simmering water, for 2 hours. Unwrap and serve hot, with custard sauce, cream, or ice cream.

'SUSSEX POND PUDDING'

¾ cup (1½ sticks) butter, plus
extra for greasing
1 lemon, scrubbed
1 cup sugar
sour cream or crème fraîche
for serving

suet dough
1¼ cups all-purpose flour
⅓ cup butter
⅓ cup ground or finely chopped
beef suet
½ tsp. salt
½ tsp. sugar
about 1 Tbs. warm water

Tip You could use
an orange instead of
the lemon—perhaps
a blood orange, so
you get a lovely red
color—or individual
puddings with a lime
in the center of each.

**When you make this, you will see why it is called
Sussex Pond pudding.**

Mix all the ingredients for the dough together, kneading lightly
until smooth. Try not to over-work it or the heat of your hands
will melt the suet and the crust will not be springy.

Roll out one-third of the dough into a circle large enough to cover
the top of a 1-quart ceramic pudding basin, steamed-pudding
mold, or other heatproof bowl; set side. Grease the inside of the
mold with a little butter. Cut a circle of parchment paper to fit the
bottom of the mold. Moisten it with water to make it more pliable
and press inside. Roll out the remaining dough into a circle big
enough to line the mold, leaving a small overhang around the
top. Press the dough gently into the mold.

Spike the rind of the lemon all over with a fork. Put about half of
the butter inside the mold and cover with half of the sugar, then
wedge the lemon upright in this. Cover with the remaining sugar
and butter.

Put the pastry lid on top of the pudding and bring the overhang
over the top. Moisten the underside with a little water and press
gently to seal. Cover the top of the pudding with a double sheet
of parchment paper, again moistened with water, and tie with
string to keep it in place. Finally, wrap the whole thing in foil.

Put a folded dishtowel on the bottom of a large pan and set the
mold on top. Add enough boiling water to come three-quarters of
the way up the side of the mold. Cover and steam for 2½ hours,
replenishing the water when necessary.

Remove the mold from the pan and take off the foil and paper.
Unmold the pudding and cut a big wedge for each person. Serve
hot, with sour cream or crème fraîche.

'CLOOTIE PUDDING'

½ cup warm milk

⅔ cup golden syrup or molasses

1 tsp. ground ginger

1 tsp. ground cinnamon

2 eggs, lightly beaten

1⅓ cups mixed golden raisins
   and currants

2 carrots, grated

2½ cups all-purpose flour,
   plus 1 Tbs. for the cloth

1 Tbs. baking powder

½ cup sugar

⅔ cup steel-cut Scotch oats
   (pinhead oatmeal)

1 cup ground or finely chopped
   beef suet

vanilla custard sauce (recipe on
   page 240) for serving

This is the Scottish version of plum pudding, wrapped in a cloth for cooking rather than being steamed in a mold. It has many variations—for example, with grated apples instead of carrots, or with a lot more spicing. The traditional way to serve it is to cool it, cut it into slices or wedges, pour custard sauce over it, and bake, which produces a baked custard-pudding-stodgy-dumpling thing. Well, the Scots have to keep warm somehow, don't they?

Warm the milk in a large saucepan. Add the golden syrup, or molasses, and spices, then take the pan off the heat. When it's coolish, add the beaten eggs, dried fruit, and grated carrots.

Sift together the flour and baking powder, then add the sugar, oats, and suet. Rub together until well combined. Add the wet ingredients to the dry and mix well together.

Lay a thick, clean cloth on the work surface. Pile the mixture into the middle and wrap it up into a bundle, tying at the top with kitchen string. Cook in a steamer over boiling water for about 3 hours, then take the pudding out and let cool.

Heat the oven to 325°F. Cut the pudding into slices, put them in a baking dish, and cover with the custard sauce. Bake until bubbling and golden brown on top, about 30 minutes.

'SWEET POPOVERS WITH PLUM JAM & CLOTTED CREAM'

jam
4 lb. plums
2½ cups water
4 lb. sugar

clotted cream
3 cups heavy cream (not
  ultrapasteurized)
2 Tbs. butter
1 vanilla bean (optional)

popovers
8 eggs
2½ cups milk
3½ cups all-purpose flour, sifted
3 Tbs. beef drippings
confectioners' sugar, sifted

Clotted cream is traditionally served with scones and jam for an English "cream tea," although it is just as irresistible spooned onto any plain cake or fruit dessert. Not always easy to buy, this is how to make some at home. The jam recipe makes about 6 pounds; if you prefer, use a bought jam (raspberry is good).

To make the jam, wash the plums and cut them in half. Put them, with their pits, into a large pan with the water and simmer gently until soft. Add the sugar and stir until it dissolves.

Bring the jam to a boil, removing any pits and froth as they rise to the surface, and boil rapidly. To test for doneness, remove from the heat, then put a blob of jam on a chilled plate and refrigerate for a few minutes—the jam is done if the surface wrinkles when you push your finger into the blob.

When the jam is ready, skim, then ladle into sterilized jars and seal. (For long storage, process in a boiling-water bath.)

To make the clotted cream, mix the cream and butter in a heavy pan and bring to a simmer over medium heat. Stir constantly with a wooden spoon. About 8 minutes later, the volume of cream should be almost half what it was when you started. If using the vanilla bean, add it toward the end of the simmering process. Pour the cream into a shallow bowl and refrigerate.

To make the popovers, heat the oven to 425°F. Beat the eggs with the milk, then beat in the flour to make a batter. Put a popover tin or muffin pan in the oven until hot. Add some drippings to each hole and heat until the fat is smoking-hot. Ladle some batter into each hole, then return the tin or pan to the oven. Reduce the heat to 400°F and bake for 15 minutes.

Take the popovers from the oven and put one on each serving plate. Top each popover with a big spoonful of jam and some clotted cream. Dust with confectioners' sugar and serve hot.

'INDEX'

250

'EQUIVALENCY CHARTS'

OVEN TEMPERATURES

Gas Mark	°F	°C
1/2	250	120
1	275	140
2	300	150
3	325	165
4	350	180
5	375	190
6	400	200
7	425	220
8	450	230
9	475	240
10	500	260
Broil	550	290

LIQUID/DRY MEASURES

U.S.	Metric
1/4 teaspoon	1.25 milliliters
1/2 teaspoon	2.5 milliliters
1 teaspoon	5 milliliters
1 tablespoon (3 teaspoons)	15 milliliters
1 fluid ounce (2 tablespoons)	30 milliliters
1/4 cup	60 milliliters
1/3 cup	80 milliliters
1/2 cup	120 milliliters
1 cup	240 milliliters
1 pint (2 cups)	480 milliliters
1 quart (4 cups; 32 ounces)	960 milliliters
1 gallon (4 quarts)	3.84 liters
1 ounce (by weight)	28 grams
1 pound	454 grams
2.2 pounds	1 kilogram

'BEEF SOURCES'

Allen Brothers, Inc.
3737 S. Halsted St.
Chicago, IL 60609-1689
(800) 548-7777
www.allenbrothers.com

Bell Creek Beef
5935 McCall Lane
Arlington, NE 68002
(877) 235-5273
www.bellcreekbeef.com

Brandt Beef
P.O. Box 118
Brawley, CA 92227
www.brandtbeef.com

Cusack Meats
301 S.W. 12th St.
Oklahoma City, OK 73109
(800) 241-6328
www.cusackmeats.com

James River Meat Company
P.O. Box 95
Manakin-Sabot, VA 23103
(877) 313-5695
www.jamesrivermeat.com

Kansas City Steak Company
100 Osage Ave.
Kansas City, KS 66105
(800) 524-1844
www.kansascitysteaks.com

Lobel's of New York
1096 Madison Ave.
New York, NY 10028
(877) 783-4512
www.lobels.com

Morgan Ranch
83583 Gracie Creek Ave.
Burwell, NE 68823
(308) 346-4394
www.morganranchinc.com

My Butcher
www.mybutcher.com

New Brunswick Steak Co.
Milltown, NJ 08850
(908) 307-3608
www.newbrunswicksteakco.com

Niman Ranch
(866) 808-0340
www.nimanranch.com

Omaha Steaks
10909 John Galt Blvd.
P.O. Box 3300
Omaha, NE 68103
(800) 228-9872
www.omahasteaks.com

PrimeChops.Com
2538 E. 53rd St
Huntington Park, CA 90255
(619) 222-0174
www.primechops.com

S & S Meat Company
637 Prospect Ave.
Kansas City, MO 64124
(800) 800-4707
www.steaksanywhere.com

U.S. Beef
www.unitedstatesbeef.com

Wilson & Wilson Premium Steaks
(866) 596-0990
www.wilsonsteaks.com

GRASS-FED BEEF

American Grass Fed Beef
HC4 Box 253
Doniphan, MO 63935
(866) 255-5002
www.americangrassfedbeef.com

Diamond F Brand Beef, LLC
3351 State Highway 15 South
Monte Vista, CO 81144
(719) 852-2458
www.grassfedandhealthy.com

Hardwick Beef
(413) 477-6500
www.hardwickbeef.com

'ACKNOWLEDGMENTS'

La Cense Beef, LLC
945 N. Montana St.
Dillon, MT 59725
(866) 255-4985
www.lacensebeef.com

Lasater Grasslands Beef LLC
(866) 454-2333
www.lasatergrasslandsbeef.com

Slanker's Grass-Fed Meats
3255 CR 45400
Powderly, TX 75473
(866) 752-6537
www.texasgrassfedbeef.com

Tallgrass Beef Company, LLC
103 E. Main St., Suite 1
Sedan, KS 67361
(877) 822-8283
www.tallgrassbeef.com

U.S. Wellness Meats
P.O. Box 9
Monticello, MO 63457
(877) 383-0051
www.grasslandbeef.com

West Wind Farms
155 Shekinah Way
Deer Lodge, TN 37726
(423) 965-3334
www.grassorganic.com

There would be no book without the cook, and to make that cook there has been many a patient mentor. To you all—and you know who you are—thank you. To Mark Harper, a man who laughs at my ridiculous ideas, but then makes my dreams a reality: YOU ROCK. That poster boy is the best. ☛ For Claire Peters, who while designing this great book, was converted to eating beef. For all your time and what is a beautiful book, thanks. To Jenni Muir, the straight-faced editor with a big heart and great mind: patience is a virtue and by God you're virtuous, and sometimes funny! This is a great book because of your pestering and care. Thank you. Without the persistence of Anne Furniss, Alison Cathie, Helen Lewis, and the team at Quadrille, this book would not be, either. Thanks for believing that a single-subject book is a good thing. ☛ For all my team at Smiths of Smithfield: you are the best of the best and Smiths is all down to you. Special thanks to one man in particular, Tony Moyse—without you this book would not be, and without you Smiths would not be what it is. You are a fab man (and thanks for letting him out, Claire). ☛ To Jessie, my missus, who made the rambling words of a mad chef into language the world would understand, and for keeping me in it. Thanks, Beautiful. ☛ There is also this guy who takes great photos. His name is Jason Lowe and he is really, really good. I love working with you, Jason, but next time I will insist on the watercress. The throne works as you said it would! Big ones. ☛ For all the team at *Masterchef*, in particular Gregg Wallace and his big bald head, and the lovely, trusting, believing Karen Ross. Thanks for making me famous. Sometimes I like it. ☛ In this great restaurant industry, we all learn by copying each other, so thanks to all the people I have worked with and who have inspired me. ☛ Lastly, to every farmer, butcher, producer, and grower—without your knowledge and love of what you do, and the lessons you have taught me, without you there would be no **BEEF**!

The Taunton Press
Inspiration for hands-on living®

The Taunton Press, Inc.
63 South Main Street, PO Box 5506
Newtown, CT 06470-5506
www.taunton.com

First published in 2008 by
Quadrille Publishing Limited
Alhambra House
27-31 Charing Cross Road
London WC2H OLS
www.quadrille.co.uk

Text © 2008 John Torode
Photography © 2008 Jason Lowe
Design and layout © 2008 Quadrille Publishing Ltd
The rights of the author have been asserted.

Editorial Director Anne Furniss
Creative Director Helen Lewis
Project Editor Jenni Muir
US Editor Norma MacMillan
Designer Claire Peters
Design Consultant Mark Harper
Photographer Jason Lowe
Props Styling Cynthia Inions
Food Stylists John Torode and
  Tony Moyse
Production Ruth Deary

Library of Congress Cataloging-in-Publication Data

Torode, John.
  Beef / John Torode ; photographer, Jason Lowe
Quadrille.
    p. cm.
  Originally published: London : Quadrille Pub. Ltd.,
2008.
  Includes index.
  ISBN 978-1-60085-126-1
  1. Cookery (Beef) I. Title.
  TX749.5.B43T67 2009
  641.3'62—dc22

                            2008036515

Printed in China